The Pleasant Comedy of Old Fortunatus by Thomas Dekker

Thomas Dekker was a playwright, pamphleteer and poet who, perhaps, deserves greater recognition than he has so far gained.

Despite the fact only perhaps twenty of his plays were published, and fewer still survive, he was far more prolific than that. Born around 1572 his peak years were the mid 1590's to the 1620's – seven of which he spent in a debtor's prison. His works span the late Elizabethan and Caroline eras and his numerous collaborations with Ford, Middleton, Webster and Jonson say much about his work.

His pamphlets detail much of the life in these times, times of great change, of plague and of course that great capital city London a swirling mass of people, power, intrigue.

Index of Contents
PREFACE
THE PROLOGUE AT COURT
PROLOGUE
DRAMATIS PERSONÆ
SCENE—CYPRUS, BABYLON, and ENGLAND
OLD FORTUNATUS
ACT THE FIRST
SCENE I.—A Wood in Cyprus
SCENE II.—Outside the House of Fortunatus
SCENE III.—A Wood in Cyprus
ACT THE SECOND
SCENE I.—The Court at Babylon
SCENE II.—Outside the House of Fortunatus
ACT THE THIRD
SCENE I.—London. The Court of Athelstane
SCENE II.—The Same
ACT THE FOURTH
SCENE I.—A Wilderness
SCENE II.—London. The Court of Athelstane
ACT THE FIFTH
SCENE I.—London. The Court of Athelstane
SCENE II.—An open Space near London: a Prison and a Pair of Stocks in the background
THE EPILOGUE AT COURT
THOMAS DEKKER – A SHORT BIOGRAPHY
THOMAS DEKKER – A CONCISE BIBLIOGRAPHY

PREFACE

The Pleasant Comedy of Old Fortunatus was first published in 1600, having been produced at Court on the Christmas before. The play as it stands is an amplification and a recast of an earlier play, The First Part of Fortunatus, which had been performed at Henslowe's Theatre about four years previously. This had long been laid aside, when the idea seems to have occurred to Henslowe to revive it in fuller form, and Dekker was commissioned to write a second part, with the result that he recast the whole in one play instead, adding the episode of the sons of Fortunatus to the original version. So far, the whole play was taken from the same source, the old Volksbuch of "Fortunatus," which, first published at Augsburg in 1509, was popular in various languages in the sixteenth century. An interesting account of this legend and of its connection with the play, is given in Professor Herford's "Studies in the Literary Relations of England and Germany in the Sixteenth Century," from which the present note on the play is largely drawn. When Dekker had completed his recast of the play, it was immediately ordered for performance at Court, and further scenes, in this case altogether extraneous to the original story—those, namely, in which Virtue and Vice are introduced as rivals to Fortune—were added with a special view to this end. Otherwise the play is pretty faithful to the story, even in its absurdities. It is worth mention that Hans Sachs had already dramatized the subject in 1553, which may have had something to do indirectly with the production of the first English version.

In the original quarto of 1600, Old Fortunatus is not divided into acts and scenes, and the division is here attempted for the first time. It has been necessary also in some instances to supply stage directions.

THE PROLOGUE AT COURT.[1]

[1] This Prologue and the Epilogue are specially devised for the performance of the play before the queen, hence "At Court."

Enter TWO OLD MEN.

1st OLD MAN
Are you then travelling to the temple of Eliza?[2]

[2] i.e. Queen Elizabeth, at this time in her sixty-eighth year.

Pandora is the only one of these poetic terms for Elizabeth peculiar to Dekker. The rest of them are used by others of the Elizabethan poets. He evidently here conceives Pandora on the side of her good fortune only, as receiving the gifts of the gods, and not in her more familiar association with the story of Pandora's Box and its evils.

2nd OLD MAN
Even to her temple are my feeble limbs travelling. Some call her Pandora: some Gloriana, some Cynthia: some Delphœbe, some Astræa: all by several names to express several loves: yet all those names make but one celestial body, as all those loves meet to create but one soul.

1st OLD MAN
I am one of her own country, and we adore her by the name of Eliza.

2nd OLD MAN
Blessed name, happy country: your Eliza makes your land Elysium: but what do you offer?

1st OLD MAN
That which all true subjects should: when I was young, an armed hand; now I am crooked, an upright heart: but what offer you?

2nd OLD MAN
That which all strangers do: two eyes struck blind with admiration: two lips proud to sound her glory: two hands held up full of prayers and praises: what not, that may express love? what not, that may make her beloved?

1st OLD MAN
How long is't since you last beheld her?

2nd OLD MAN
A just year: yet that year hath seemed to me but one day, because her glory hath been my hourly contemplation, and yet that year hath seemed to me more than twice seven years, because so long I have been absent from her. Come therefore, good father, let's go faster, lest we come too late: for see, the tapers of the night are already lighted, and stand brightly burning in their starry candle-sticks: see how gloriously the moon shines upon us. [Both kneel.

1st OLD MAN
Peace, fool: tremble, and kneel: the moon say'st thou?
Our eyes are dazzled by Eliza's beams,
See (if at least thou dare see) where she sits:
This is the great Pantheon of our goddess,
And all those faces which thine eyes thought stars,
Are nymphs attending on her deity.
Prithee begin, for I want power to speak.

2nd OLD MAN
No, no, speak thou, I want words to begin.

[Weeps.

1st OLD MAN
Alack, what shall I do? com'st thou with me,
And weep'st now thou behold'st this majesty?

2nd OLD MAN
Great landlady of hearts, pardon me.

1st OLD MAN
Blame not mine eyes, good father, in these tears.

2nd OLD MAN
My pure love shines, as thine doth in thy fears:
I weep for joy to see so many heads
Of prudent ladies, clothed in the livery

Of silver-handed age, for serving you,
Whilst in your eyes youth's glory doth renew:
I weep for joy to see the sun look old,
To see the moon mad at her often change,
To see the stars only by night to shine,
Whilst you are still bright, still one, still divine:
I weep for joy to see the world decay,
Yet see Eliza flourishing like May:
O pardon me your pilgrim, I have measured
Many a mile to find you: and have brought
Old Fortunatus and his family,
With other Cypriots, my poor countrymen,
To pay a whole year's tribute: O vouchsafe,
Dread Queen of Fairies, with your gracious eyes,
T'accept theirs and our humble sacrifice.

1st OLD MAN
Now I'll beg for thee too: and yet I need not:
Her sacred hand hath evermore been known,
As soon held out to strangers as her own.

2nd OLD MAN
Thou dost encourage me: I'll fetch them in,
They have no princely gifts, we are all poor,
Our offerings are true hearts, who can wish more?

[Exeunt.

PROLOGUE

Of Love's sweet war our timorous Muse doth sing,
And to the bosom of each gentle dear,
Offers her artless tunes, borne on the wing
Of sacred poesy. A benumbing fear,
That your nice souls, cloyed with delicious sounds,
Will loath her lowly notes, makes her pull in
Her fainting pinions, and her spirit confounds,
Before the weak voice of her song begin.
Yet since within the circle of each eye,
Being like so many suns in his round sphere,
No wrinkle yet is seen, she'll dare to fly,
Borne up with hopes, that as you oft do rear
With your fair hands, those who would else sink down,
So some will deign to smile, where all might frown:
And for this small circumference must stand,
For the imagined surface of much land,

Of many kingdoms, and since many a mile
Should here be measured out, our Muse entreats
Your thoughts to help poor art, and to allow
That I may serve as Chorus to her senses;
She begs your pardon, for she'll send one forth,
Not when the laws of poesy do call,
But as the story needs; your gracious eye
Gives life to Fortunatus' history.

[Exit.

DRAMATIS PERSONÆ.

ATHELSTANE, King of England.
The Soldan of Egypt.
The Prince of Cyprus.
CORNWALL,   }
CHESTER,   } English Nobles.
LINCOLN,   }
MONTROSE,   } Scotch Nobles.
GALLOWAY,   }
ORLEANS,   } French Nobles.
LONGAVILLE,   }
INSULTADO, a Spanish Lord.
FORTUNATUS.
AMPEDO,   } Sons of FORTUNATUS.
ANDELOCIA,   }
SHADOW, Servant to AMPEDO and ANDELOCIA.
Kings, Nobles, Soldiers, Satyrs, a Carter, a Tailor, a Monk, a Shepherd,
Chorus, Boys and other Attendants.
AGRIPYNE, Daughter of ATHELSTANE.
FORTUNE,   }
VIRTUE,   } Goddesses.
VICE,   }
The Three Destinies.
Nymphs, Ladies, &c.

SCENE—CYPRUS, BABYLON, and ENGLAND.

OLD FORTUNATUS.

ACT THE FIRST.

SCENE I.—A Wood in Cyprus.

Enter FORTUNATUS meanly attired; he walks about cracking nuts ere he speaks.

FORTUNATUS
So, ho, ho, ho, ho.

ECHO [Within.]
Ho, ho, ho, ho.

FORTUNATUS
There, boy.

ECHO
There, boy.

FORTUNATUS
An thou bee'st a good fellow, tell me how call'st this wood.

ECHO
This wood.

FORTUNATUS
Ay, this wood, and which is my best way out.

ECHO
Best way out.

FORTUNATUS
Ha, ha, ha, that's true, my best way out is my best way out, but how that out will come in, by this maggot I know not. I see by this we are all worms' meat. Well, I am very poor and very patient; Patience is a virtue: would I were not virtuous, that's to say, not poor, but full of vice, that's to say, full of chinks. Ha, ha, so I am, for I am so full of chinks, that a horse with one eye may look through and through me. I have sighed long, and that makes me windy; I have fasted long, and that makes me chaste; marry, I have prayed little, and that makes me I still dance in this conjuring circle; I have wandered long, and that makes me weary. But for my weariness, anon I'll lie down, instead of fasting I'll feed upon nuts, and instead of sighing will laugh and be lean, Sirrah Echo.

ECHO
Sirrah Echo.

FORTUNATUS
Here's a nut.

ECHO
Here's a nut.

FORTUNATUS
Crack it.

ECHO
Crack it.

FORTUNATUS
Hang thyself.

ECHO
Hang thyself.

FORTUNATUS
Th'art a knave, a knave.

ECHO
A knave, a knave.

FORTUNATUS
Ha, ha, ha, ha!

ECHO
Ha, ha, ha, ha!

FORTUNATUS
Why so, two fools laugh at one another, I at my tittle tattle gammer Echo, and she at me. Shortly there will creep out in print some filthy book of the old hoary wandering knight, meaning me: would I were that book, for then I should be sure to creep out from hence. I should be a good soldier, for I traverse my ground rarely; marry I see neither enemy nor friends, but popinjays, and squirrels, and apes, and owls, and daws, and wagtails, and the spite is that none of these grass-eaters can speak my language, but this fool that mocks me, and swears to have the last word, in spite of my teeth, ay, and she shall have it because she is a woman, which kind of cattle are indeed all echo, nothing but tongue, and are like the great bell of St. Michael's[3] in Cyprus, that keeps most rumbling when men would most sleep. Echo, a pox on thee for mocking me.

[3] Probably a church in Famagosta, which tradition makes Fortunatus's native place, and which was at one time the chief port and fortress in Cyprus.

ECHO
A pox on thee for mocking me.

FORTUNATUS
Why so, Snip snap, this war is at an end, but this wilderness is world without end. To see how travel can transform: my teeth are turned into nutcrackers, a thousand to one I break out shortly, for I am full of nothing but waxen kernels, my tongue speaks no language but an almond for a parrot, and crack me this nut. If I hop three days more up and down this cage of cuckoos' nests, I shall turn wild man sure, and be hired to throw squibs among the commonalty upon some terrible day. In the meantime, to tell truth, here will I lie.
Farewell, fool!

ECHO

Farewell, fool.

FORTUNATUS
Are not these comfortable words to a wise man? All hail, signor tree, by your leave I'll sleep under your leaves. I pray bow to me, and I'll bend to you, for your back and my brows must, I doubt, have a game or two at noddy ere I wake again: down, great heart, down. Hey, ho, well, well. [He lies down and sleeps.

Enter a SHEPHERD, a CARTER,[4] a TAILOR,[5] and a MONK, all crowned; a NYMPH with a globe, another with FORTUNE'S wheel; then FORTUNE. After her, four KINGS with broken crowns and sceptres, chained in silver gyves and led by her. The foremost enter singing.

FORTUNE takes her chair, the KINGS lying at her feet so that she treads on them as she ascends to her seat.

[4] "A gardener" in the original, which does not tally with the description given by Fortune on p. 300. q.v.

[5] "A smith" in the original, which is again a confusion with the description in the text.

SONG.

Fortune smiles, cry holiday,
Dimples on her cheeks do dwell,
Fortune frowns, cry welladay,
Her love is Heaven, her hate is Hell:
Since Heaven and Hell obey her power.
Tremble when her eyes do lower,
Since Heaven and Hell her power obey,
When she smiles, cry holiday.
Holiday with joy we cry
And bend, and bend, and merrily
Sing hymns to Fortune's deity,
Sing hymns to Fortune's deity.

CHORUS
Let us sing, merrily, merrily, merrily,
With our song let Heaven resound,
Fortune's hands our heads have crowned;
Let us sing merrily, merrily, merrily.

1st KING
Accursed Queen of chance, what had we done,
Who having sometimes like young Phaeton,
Rid in the burnished chariot of the sun,
And sometimes been thy minions, when thy fingers
Weaved wanton love-nets in our curlèd hair,
And with sweet juggling kisses warmed our cheeks:
Oh how have we offended thy proud eyes,
That thus we should be spurned and trod upon,

Whilst those infected limbs of the sick world,
Are fixed by thee for stars in that bright sphere,
Wherein our sun-like radiance did appear.

THE KINGS
Accursèd Queen of chance, damned sorceress.

THE OTHERS
Most powerful Queen of chance, dread sovereigness.

FORTUNE
No more: curse on! your cries to me are music,
And fill the sacred rondure of mine ears
With tunes more sweet than moving of the spheres:
Curse on: on our celestial brows do sit
Unnumbered smiles, which then leap from their throne,
When they see peasants dance and monarchs groan.
Behold you not this globe, this golden bowl,
This toy called world, at our imperial feet?
This world is Fortune's ball, wherewith she sports.
Sometimes I strike it up into the air,
And then create I emperors and kings:
Sometimes I spurn it, at which spurn crawls out
That wild beast Multitude. Curse on, you fools,—
'Tis I that tumble princes from their thrones,
And gild false brows with glittering diadems.
'Tis I that tread on necks of conquerors,
And when, like demi-gods, they have been drawn
In ivory chariots to the capitol,
Circled about with wonder of all eyes,
The shouts of every tongue, love of all hearts,
Being swoll'n with their own greatness, I have pricked
The bladder of their pride, and made them die,
As water-bubbles, without memory.
I thrust base cowards into Honour's chair,
Whilst the true-spirited soldier stands by
Bare-headed, and all bare, whilst at his scars
They scoff, that ne'er durst view the face of wars.
I set an idiot's cap on Virtue's head,[6]
Turn Learning out of doors, clothe Wit in rags,
And paint ten thousand images of loam
In gaudy silken colours. On the backs
Of mules and asses I make asses ride,
Only for sport, to see the apish world
Worship such beasts with sound idolatry.
This Fortune does, and when this is done,
She sits and smiles to hear some curse her name,
And some with adoration crown her fame.

[6] An allusion to the coxcomb, the invariable ornament to the fool's cap, which Virtue wears on her head. See description, Scene III.

MONK
True centre of this wide circumference,
Sacred commandress of the destinies,
Our tongues shall only sound thy excellence.

THE OTHERS
Thy excellence our tongues shall only sound.

2nd KING
Thou painted strumpet, that with honeyed smiles,
Openest the gates of Heaven and criest, "Come in;"
Whose glories being seen, thou with one frown,
In pride, lower than hell tumblest us down.

THE KINGS
Ever, for ever, will we ban thy name.

FORTUNE
How sweet your howlings relish in mine ears!

[She comes down.

Stand by! now rise,—behold, here lies a wretch,
To vex your souls, this beggar I'll advance
Beyond the sway of thought; take instruments,
And let the raptures of choice harmony,
Thorough the hollow windings of his ear,
Carry their sacred sounds, and wake each sense,
To stand amazed at our bright eminence.

[Music. FORTUNATUS wakes.

FORTUNATUS
Oh, how am I transported? Is this earth?
Or blest Elysium?

FORTUNE
Fortunatus, rise.

FORTUNATUS
Dread goddess, how should such a wretch as I
Be known to such a glorious deity?
Oh pardon me: for to this place I come,
Led by my fate, not folly; in this wood

With weary sorrow have I wanderèd,
And three times seen the sweating sun take rest,
And three times frantic Cynthia naked ride
About the rusty highways of the skies
Stuck full of burning stars, which lent her light
To court her negro paramour grim Night.

FORTUNE
This travel now expires: yet from this circle,
Where I and these with fairy troops abide,
Thou canst not stir, unless I be thy guide.
I the world's empress am, Fortune my name,
This hand hath written in thick leaves of steel
An everlasting book of changeless fate,
Showing who's happy, who unfortunate.

FORTUNATUS
If every name, dread queen, be there writ down
I am sure mine stands in characters of black;
Though happiness herself lie in my name,
I am Sorrow's heir, and eldest son to Shame.

THE KINGS
No, we are sons to Shame, and Sorrow's heirs.

FORTUNE
Thou shalt be one of Fortune's minions:
Behold these four chained like Tartarian slaves,
These I created emperors and kings,
And these are now my basest underlings:
This sometimes was a German emperor,
Henry the Fifth,[7] who being first deposed,
Was after thrust into a dungeon,
And thus in silver chains shall rot to death.
This Frederick Barbarossa, Emperor
Of Almaine[8] once: but by Pope Alexander[9]
Now spurned and trod on when he takes his horse,
And in these fetters shall he die his slave.
This wretch once wore the diadem of France,
Lewis the meek,[10] but through his children's pride,
Thus have I caused him to be famishèd.
Here stands the very soul of misery,
Poor Bajazet, old Turkish Emperor,
And once the greatest monarch in the East;[11]
Fortune herself is said to view thy fall,
And grieves to see thee glad to lick up crumbs
At the proud feet of that great Scythian swain,
Fortune's best minion, warlike Tamburlaine:

Yet must thou in a cage of iron be drawn
In triumph at his heels, and there in grief
Dash out thy brains.

[7] The description corresponds rather to Henry IV. Of Germany, who died in 1106.

[8] Frederick I. called Barbarossa, Emperor of Germany, i.e. Allemagne (Almaine), the grandson of Henry IV.

[9] Alexander III.

[10] Louis I. called Le Débonnaire, son of Charlemagne, d. 840.

[11] Bajazet I. called Yilderim, i.e. Lightning, because of the rapidity of his movement in the field of war, first Sultan of the Ottoman Empire, who was humiliated by Timur (Tamburlaine). Compare Marlowe's Tamburlaine the Great.

4th KING
Oh miserable me!

FORTUNE
No tears can melt the heart of destiny:
These have I ruined and exalted those.
These hands have conquered Spain, these brows fill up
The golden circle of rich Portugal,—
Viriat a monarch now, but born a shepherd;[12]
This Primislaus, a Bohemian king,
Last day a carter;[13] this monk, Gregory,[14]
Now lifted to the Papal dignity;—
Wretches,[15] why gnaw you not your fingers off,
And tear your tongues out, seeing yourselves trod down,
And this Dutch botcher[16] wearing Munster's crown,
John Leyden,[17] born in Holland poor and base,
Now rich in empery and Fortune's grace?
As these I have advanced, so will I thee.
Six gifts I spend upon mortality,
Wisdom, strength, health, beauty, long life, and riches,
Out of my bounty: one of these is thine,—
Choose then which likes thee best.

[12] Viriathus, a shepherd who became a famous Lusitanian chief in the 2nd century B.C., and long warred successfully against the Romans in Spain.

[13] Primislaus, a country labourer, who became first Duke of Bohemia, having married the daughter of Croc who founded the city of Prague.

[14] Gregory VII. (1013-1085).

[15] Fortune here turns and addresses the four deposed kings again.

[16] Tailor. See The Devil's Answer to Pierce Pennylesse (Dekker's non-dramatic works, The Huth Library, edited by the Rev. A. B. Grosart, vol. ii. p. 147), "That botcher I preferred to be Lucifer's tailor, because he works with a hot needle and burnt thread."

[17] John of Leyden (John Beccold), b. 1510, d. 1536, a tailor, who became a leader of the Anabaptists and at their head took extraordinary possession of the city of Munster, and ruled for a brief space as king there, before constitutional authority was restored and he was seized and put to death.

FORTUNATUS
Oh most divine!
Give me but leave to borrow wonder's eye,
To look amazed at thy bright majesty,
Wisdom, strength, health, beauty, long life, and riches.

FORTUNE
Before thy soul at this deep lottery
Draw forth her prize, ordained by destiny,
Know that here's no recanting a first choice.
Choose then discreetly for the laws of Fate,
Being graven in steel, must stand inviolate.

FORTUNATUS
Daughters of Jove and the unblemished Night,
Most righteous Parcae,[18] guide my genius right,
Wisdom, strength, health, beauty, long life, and riches.

[18] The Three Destinies, to whom Fortune herself was sometimes added as a fourth. Fortunatus here seems to be addressing Fortune and her two attendant nymphs, for no stage direction is specially given for the entrance of the Three Destinies, as in Act II. sc. ii., q.v.

FORTUNE
Stay, Fortunatus, once more hear me speak;
If thou kiss Wisdom's cheek and make her thine,
She'll breathe into thy lips divinity,
And thou like Phœbus shalt speak oracle,
Thy Heaven-inspired soul, on Wisdom's wings,
Shall fly up to the Parliament of Jove,
And read the statutes of eternity,
And see what's past and learn what is to come.
If thou lay claim to strength, armies shall quake
To see thee frown: as kings at mine do lie,
So shall thy feet trample on empery.
Make health thine object, thou shalt be strong proof
'Gainst the deep searching darts of surfeiting,
Be ever merry, ever revelling.
Wish but for beauty, and within thine eyes

Two naked Cupids amorously shall swim,[19]
And on thy cheeks I'll mix such white and red,
That Jove shall turn away young Ganymede,
And with immortal arms shall circle thee.
Are thy desires long life?—thy vital thread
Shall be stretched out, thou shalt behold the change
Of monarchies and see those children die,
Whose great great grandsires now in cradles lie.
If through gold's sacred hunger thou dost pine,
Those gilded wantons which in swarms do run,
To warm their tender bodies in the sun,
Shall stand for number of those golden piles,
Which in rich pride shall swell before thy feet;
As those are, so shall these be infinite.
Awaken then thy soul's best faculties,
And gladly kiss this bounteous hand of Fate,
Which strives to bless thy name of Fortunate.

[19] See an anonymous poem in Tottel's Miscellany, 1557, called "A praise of his Lady," from which Dekker may have borrowed the fancy:—

"In each of her two crystal eyes
Smileth a naked boy."

THE KINGS
Old man, take heed, her smiles will murder thee.

THE OTHERS
Old man, she'll crown thee with felicity.

FORTUNATUS
Oh, whither am I rapt beyond myself?
More violent conflicts fight in every thought,
Than his whose fatal choice Troy's downfall wrought.
Shall I contract myself to wisdom's love?
Then I lose riches: and a wise man poor,
Is like a sacred book that's never read,—
To himself he lives, and to all else seems dead.
This age thinks better of a gilded fool,
Than of a threadbare saint in wisdom's school.
I will be strong: then I refuse long life,
And though mine arm should conquer twenty worlds,
There's a lean fellow beats all conquerors:
The greatest strength expires with loss of breath;
The mightiest in one minute stoop to death.
Then take long life, or health: should I do so
I might grow ugly, and that tedious scroll
Of months and years, much misery may enroll

Therefore I'll beg for beauty; yet I will not,
That fairest cheek hath oftentimes a soul
Leprous as sin itself; than hell more foul.
The wisdom of this world is idiotism,
Strength a weak reed: health sickness' enemy,
And it at length will have the victory.
Beauty is but a painting, and long life
Is a long journey in December gone,
Tedious and full of tribulation.
Therefore, dread sacred Empress, make me rich,

[Kneels down.

My choice is store of gold; the rich are wise.
He that upon his back rich garments wears,
Is wise, though on his head grow Midas' ears.
Gold is the strength, the sinews of the world,
The health, the soul, the beauty most divine,
A mask of gold hides all deformities;
Gold is Heaven's physic, life's restorative,
Oh therefore make me rich: not as the wretch,
That only serves lean banquets to his eye,
Has gold, yet starves: is famished in his store:
No, let me ever spend, be never poor.

FORTUNE
Thy latest words confine thy destiny,
Thou shalt spend ever, and be never poor:
For proof receive this purse: with it this virtue
Still when thou thrust thy hand into the same,
Thou shalt draw forth ten pieces of bright gold,
Current in any realm where then thou breathest;
If thou canst dribble out the sea by drops,
Then shalt thou want: but that can ne'er be done,
Nor this grow empty.

FORTUNATUS
Thanks, great deity.

FORTUNE
The virtue ends when thou and thy sons end.
This path leads thee to Cyprus,[20] get thee hence;
Farewell, vain covetous fool, thou wilt repent,
That for the love of dross thou hast despised
Wisdom's divine embrace, she would have borne thee
On the rich wings of immortality;
But now go dwell with cares and quickly die.

[20] Dekker is not careful even to remember here that Cyprus is an island.

THE KINGS
We dwell with cares, yet cannot quickly die.

[Exeunt all singing, except FORTUNATUS.

FORTUNATUS
But now go dwell with cares and quickly die. How quickly? if I die to-morrow, I'll be merry to-day: if next day, I'll be merry to-morrow. Go dwell with cares? Where dwells Care? Hum ha, in what house dwells Care, that I may choose an honester neighbour? In princes' courts? No. Among fair ladies? Neither: there's no care dwells with them, but care how to be most gallant. Among gallants then? Fie, fie, no! Care is afraid sure of a gilt rapier, the scent of musk is her prison, tobacco chokes her, rich attire presseth her to death. Princes, fair ladies and gallants, have amongst you then, for this wet-eyed wench Care dwells with wretches: they are wretches that feel want, I shall feel none if I be never poor; therefore, Care, I cashier you my company. I wonder what blind gossip this minx is that is so prodigal; she should be a good one by her open dealing: her name's Fortune: it's no matter what she is, so she does as she says. "Thou shalt spend ever, and be never poor." Mass, yet I feel nothing here to make me rich:—here's no sweet music with her silver sound. Try deeper: ho God be here: ha, ha, one, two, three, four, five, six, seven, eight, nine and ten, good, just ten. It's so heavy, try again, one, two, &c. Good again, just ten, and just ten. Ha, ha, ha, this is rare: a leather mint, admirable: an Indian mine in a lamb's skin, miraculous! I'll fill three or four bags full for my sons, but keep this for myself. If that lean tawny face tobacconist Death, that turns all into smoke, must turn me so quickly into ashes, yet I will not mourn in ashes, but in music, hey, old lad, be merry. Here's riches, wisdom, strength, health, beauty, and long life (if I die not quickly). Sweet purse, I kiss thee; Fortune, I adore thee; Care, I despise thee; Death, I defy thee.[21]

[Exit.

[21] Compare Shakespeare's "Crabbed Age and Youth."

SCENE II.—Outside the House of Fortunatus.

Enter AMPEDO, SHADOW after him, both sad: then ANDELOCIA.

ANDELOCIA
'Sheart,[22] why how now: two knights of the post?[23]

[22] A corruption of "God's heart."

[23] Hired witnesses.

SHADOW
Ay, master, and we are both forsworn, as all such wooden knights be, for we both took an oath—marry it was not corporal, you may see by our cheeks, that we would not fast twenty-four hours to amend, and we have tasted no meat since the clock told two dozen.

ANDELOCIA
That lacks not much of twenty-four, but I wonder when that half-faced moon of thine will be at the full.

SHADOW
The next quarter, not this, when the sign is in Taurus.

ANDELOCIA
Ho, that's to say, when thou eat'st bull beef.
But, Shadow, what day is to-day?

SHADOW
Fasting day.

ANDELOCIA
What day was yesterday?

SHADOW
Fasting day too.

ANDELOCIA
Will to-morrow be so too?

SHADOW
Ay, and next day too.

ANDELOCIA
That will be rare, you slave:
For a lean diet makes a fat wit.

SHADOW
I had rather be a fool and wear a fat pair of cheeks.

ANDELOCIA
Now I am prouder of this poverty, which I know is mine own, than a waiting gentlewoman is of a frizzled groatsworth of hair, that never grew on her head. Sir Shadow, now we can all three swear like Puritans at one bare word: this want makes us like good bowlers, we are able to rub out and shift in every place.

SHADOW
That's not so, we have shifted ourselves in no place this three months: marry, we rub out in every corner, but here follows no amendment either of life or of livery.

ANDELOCIA
Why, brother Ampedo, art thou not yet tired with riding post? Come, come, 'light from this loggerheaded jade, and walk afoot, and talk with your poor friends.

SHADOW
Nay, by my troth, he is like me: if his belly be empty, his heart is full.

ANDELOCIA
The famine of gold gnaws his covetous stomach, more than the want of good victuals: thou hast looked very devilishly ever since the good angel[24] left thee: come, come, leave this broad-brim fashions; because the world frowns upon thee, wilt not thou smile upon us?

[24] *One of the usual puns on the coin of that name.*

AMPEDO
Did but the bitterness of mine own fortunes
Infect my taste, I could paint o'er my cheeks
With ruddy-coloured smiles: 'tis not the want
Of costly diet or desire of gold
Enforces rupture in my wounded breast.
Oh no, our father—if he live—doth lie
Under the iron foot of misery,
And, as a dove gripped in a falcon's claw,
There pant'th for life being most assured of death.
Brother, for him my soul thus languisheth.

SHADOW
'Tis not for my old master that I languish.

AMPEDO
I am not enamoured of this painted idol,
This strumpet World; for her most beauteous looks
Are poisoned baits, hung upon golden hooks:
When fools do swim in wealth, her Cynthian beams
Will wantonly dance on the silver streams;
But when this squint-eyed age sees Virtue poor,
And by a little spark sits shivering,
Begging at all, relieved at no man's door,
She smiles on her, as the sun shines on fire,
To kill that little heat, and, with her little frown,
Is proud that she can tread poor Virtue down:
Therefore her wrinkled brow makes not mine sour,
Her gifts are toys, and I desire her power.

SHADOW
'Tis not the crab-tree faced World neither that makes mine sour.

ANDELOCIA
Her gifts toys! Well, brother Virtue, we have let slip the ripe plucking of those toys so long, that we flourish like apple-trees in September, which, having the falling sickness, bear neither fruit nor leaves.

SHADOW
Nay, by my troth, master, none flourish in these withering times, but ancient bearers[25] and trumpeters.

[25] Ensign-bearers.

ANDELOCIA
Shadow, when thou provest a substance, then the tree of virtue and honesty, and such fruit of Heaven, shall flourish upon earth.

SHADOW
True; or when the sun shines at midnight, or women fly, and yet they are light enough.

ANDELOCIA
'Twas never merry world with us, since purses and bags were invented, for now men set lime-twigs to catch wealth: and gold, which riseth like the sun out of the East Indies, to shine upon every one, is like a cony taken napping in a pursenet,[26] and suffers his glistering yellow-face deity to be lapped up in lambskins, as if the innocency of those leather prisons should dispense with the cheveril[27] consciences of the iron-hearted gaolers.

[26] A net the ends of which are drawn together with a string like a purse.

[27] Kid leather (Fr. chevreau). Hence a very flexible conscience was often called a cheveril conscience.—Halliwell.

SHADOW
Snudges[28] may well be called gaolers: for if a poor wretch steal but into a debt of ten pound, they lead him straight to execution.

[28] Mean or miserly persons.—Halliwell.

ANDELOCIA
Doth it not vex thee, Shadow, to stalk up and down Cyprus, and to meet the outside of a man, lapped all in damask, his head and beard as white as milk, only with conjuring in the snowy circles of the field argent, and his nose as red as scarlet, only with kissing the ruddy lips of angels, and such an image to wear on his thumb, three men's livings in the shape of a seal ring, whilst my brother Virtue here,—

SHADOW
And you his brother Vice!

ANDELOCIA
Most true, my little lean Iniquity—whilst we three, if we should starve, cannot borrow five shillings of him neither in word nor deed: does not this vex thee, Shadow?

SHADOW
Not me; it vexes me no more to see such a picture, than to see an ass laden with riches, because I know when he can bear no longer, he must leave his burthen to some other beast.

ANDELOCIA
Art not thou mad, to see money on goldsmiths' stalls, and none in our purses?

SHADOW

It mads not me, I thank the destinies.

ANDELOCIA
By my poverty, and that's but a thread-bare oath, I am more than mad to see silks and velvets lie crowding together in mercers' shops, as in prisons, only for fear of the smell of wax—they cannot abide to see a man made out of wax, for these satin commodities have such smooth consciences that they'll have no man give his word for them or stand bound for their coming forth, but vow to lie till they rot in those shop counters, except Monsieur Money bail them. Shadow, I am out of my little wits to see this.

SHADOW
So is not Shadow: I am out of my wits, to see fat gluttons feed all day long, whilst I that am lean fast every day: I am out of my wits, to see our Famagosta fools turn half a shop of wares into a suit of gay apparel, only to make other idiots laugh, and wise men to cry, who's the fool now? I am mad, to see soldiers beg, and cowards brave: I am mad, to see scholars in the broker's shop, and dunces in the mercer's: I am mad, to see men that have no more fashion in them than poor Shadow, yet must leap thrice a day into three orders of fashions: I am mad, to see many things, but horn-mad, that my mouth feels nothing.

ANDELOCIA
Why now, Shadow, I see thou hast a substance:
I am glad to see thee thus mad.

AMPEDO
The sons of Fortunatus had not wont
Thus to repine at others' happiness:
But fools have always this loose garment wore,
Being poor themselves, they wish all others poor.
Fie, brother Andelocia, hate this madness,
Turn your eyes inward, and behold your soul,
That wants more than your body; burnish that
With glittering virtue, and make idiots grieve
To see your beauteous mind in wisdom shine,
As you at their rich poverty repine.

Enter FORTUNATUS, gallant.[29]

[29] i.e. Gallantly attired.

ANDELOCIA
Peace, good Virtue; Shadow, here comes another shadow.

SHADOW
It should be a chameleon: for he is all in colours.

AMPEDO
Oh, 'tis my father. With these tears of joy,
My love and duty greet your fair return!
A double gladness hath refreshed my soul;

One, that you live, and one, to see your fate
Looks freshly howsoever poor in state.

ANDELOCIA
My father Fortunatus, and thus brave?

SHADOW
'Tis no wonder to see a man brave, but a wonder how he comes brave.

FORTUNATUS
Dear Andelocia and son Ampedo,
And my poor servant Shadow, plume your spirits
With light-winged mirth; for Fortunatus' hand
Can now pour golden showers into their laps
That sometimes scorned him for his want of gold.
Boys, I am rich, and you shall ne'er be poor;
Wear gold, spend gold, we all in gold will feed,
Now is your father Fortunate indeed.

ANDELOCIA
Father, be not angry, if I set open the windows of my mind: I doubt for all your bragging, you'll prove like most of our gallants in Famagosta, that have a rich outside and a beggarly inside, and like mules wear gay trappings, and good velvet foot-cloths[30] on their backs, yet champ on the iron bit of penury—I mean, want coin. You gild our ears with a talk of gold, but I pray dazzle our eyes with the majesty of it.

[30] *Housings hung on horses and mules, and considered a mark of dignity.—Halliwell.*

FORTUNATUS
First will I wake your senses with the sound
Of gold's sweet music: tell me what you hear?

AMPEDO
Believe me, sir, I hear not any thing.

ANDELOCIA
Ha, ha, ha. 'Sheart, I thought as much; if I hear any jingling, but of the purse strings that go flip flap, flip flap, flip flap, would I were turned into a flip-flap,[31] and sold to the butchers!

[31] *A stick with leather flap for killing flies.*

FORTUNATUS
Shadow, I'll try thine ears; hark, dost rattle?

SHADOW
Yes, like three blue beans in a blue bladder, rattle bladder, rattle: your purse is like my belly, th' one's without money, th' other without meat.

FORTUNATUS
Bid your eyes blame the error of your ears:
You misbelieving pagans, see, here's gold—
Ten golden pieces: take them, Ampedo.
Hold, Andelocia, here are ten for thee.

AMPEDO
Shadow, there's one for thee, provide thee food.

FORTUNATUS
Stay, boy: hold, Shadow, here are ten for thee.

SHADOW
Ten, master? then defiance to fortune, and a fig for famine.

FORTUNATUS
Now tell me, wags, hath my purse gold or no?

ANDELOCIA
We the wags have gold, father; but I think there's not one angel more wagging in this sacred temple. Why, this is rare: Shadow, five will serve thy turn, give me th' other five.

SHADOW
Nay, soft, master, liberality died long ago. I see some rich beggars are never well, but when they be craving: my ten ducats are like my ten fingers, they will not jeopard a joint for you. I am yours, and these are mine; if I part from them, I shall never have part of them.

AMPEDO
Father, if Heaven have blest you once again,
Let not an open hand disperse that store,
Which gone, life's gone; for all tread down the poor.

FORTUNATUS
Peace, Ampedo, talk not of poverty.
Disdain, my boys, to kiss the tawny cheeks
Of lean necessity: make not inquiry
How I came rich; I am rich, let that suffice.
There are four leathern bags trussed full of gold:
Those spent, I'll fill you more. Go, lads, be gallant:
Shine in the streets of Cyprus like two stars,
And make them bow their knees that once did spurn you;
For, to effect such wonders, gold can turn you.
Brave it in Famagosta, or elsewhere;
I'll travel to the Turkish Emperor,
And then I'll revel it with Prester John,[32]
Or banquet with great Cham[33] of Tartary,
And try what frolic court the Soldan keeps.
I'll leave you presently. Tear off these rags;

Glitter, my boys, like angels,[34] that the world
May, whilst our life in pleasure's circle roams,
Wonder at Fortunatus and his sons.

[32] One of the followers of Ogier the Dane into India, according to Mandeville, who was given sovereignty there, and is said by tradition to have had seventy tributary kings.

[33] i.e. Khan.

[34] Another reference to the gold coins so called.

ANDELOCIA
Come, Shadow, now we'll feast it royally.

SHADOW
Do, master, but take heed of beggary.

[Exeunt.

SCENE III.—A Wood in Cyprus.

Music sounds. Enter VICE with a gilded face, and horns on her head; her garments long, painted before with silver half-moons, increasing by little and little till they come to the full; while in the midst of them is written in capital letters, "Crescit Eundo." Behind her garments are painted with fools' faces and heads; and in the midst is written, "Ha, Ha, He." She, and others wearing gilded vizards and attired like devils, bring out a fair tree of gold with apples on it.

After her comes VIRTUE, with a coxcomb on her head, and her attire all in white before; about the middle is written "Sibi sapit." Her attire behind is painted with crowns and laurel garlands, stuck full of stars held by hands thrust out of bright clouds, and among them is written, "Dominabitur astris." She and other nymphs, all in white with coxcombs on their heads, bring a tree with green and withered leaves mingled together, and with little fruit on it.

After her comes FORTUNE, with two NYMPHS, one bearing her wheel, another her globe.

And last, the PRIEST.

FORTUNE
You ministers of Virtue, Vice, and Fortune,
Tear off this upper garment of the earth,
And in her naked bosom stick these trees.

VIRTUE
How many kingdoms have I measured,
Only to find a climate, apt to cherish
These withering branches? But no ground can prove

So happy; ay me, none do Virtue love.
I'll try this soil; if here I likewise fade,
To Heaven I'll fly, from whence I took my birth,
And tell the Gods, I am banished from the earth.

VICE
Virtue, I am sworn thy foe: if there thou plant,
Here, opposite to thine, my tree shall flourish,
And as the running wood-bine spreads her arms,
To choke thy withering boughs in their embrace,
I'll drive thee from this world: were Virtue fled,
Vice as an angel should be honourèd.

FORTUNE
Servants of this bright devil and that poor saint,
Apply your task whilst you are labouring:
To make your pains seem short our priest shall sing.

[Whilst the PRIEST sings, the rest set the trees into the earth.

SONG.

Virtue's branches wither, Virtue pines,
O pity, pity, and alack the time,
Vice doth flourish, Vice in glory shines,
Her gilded boughs above the cedar climb.
Vice hath golden cheeks, O pity, pity,
She in every land doth monarchize.
Virtue is exiled from every city,
Virtue is a fool, Vice only wise.
O pity, pity, Virtue weeping dies.
Vice laughs to see her faint,—alack the time.
This sinks; with painted wings the other flies:
Alack that best should fall, and bad should climb.
O pity, pity, pity, mourn, not sing,
Vice is a saint, Virtue an underling.
Vice doth flourish, Vice in glory shines,
Virtue's branches wither, Virtue pines.

FORTUNE
Flourish or wither, Fortune cares not which,
In either's fall or height our eminence
Shines equal to the sun: the Queen of chance
Both virtuous souls and vicious doth advance.
These shadows of yourselves shall, like yourselves,
Strive to make men enamoured of their beauties;
This grove shall be our temple, and henceforth
Be consecrated to our deities.

VIRTUE
How few will come and kneel at Virtue's shrine?

VICE
This contents Virtue, that she is called divine.

FORTUNE
Poor Virtue, Fortune grieves to see thy looks
Want cunning to entice: why hang these leaves,
As loose as autumn's hair which every wind
In mockery blows from his rotten brows?
Why like a drunkard art thou pointed at?
Why is this motley-scorn[35] set on thy head?
Why stands thy court wide open, but none in it?
Why are the crystal pavements of thy temple,
Not worn, not trod upon? All is for this,
Because thy pride is to wear base attire,
Because thine eyes flame not with amorous fire.

[35] i.e. The fool's cap.

VIRTUE
Virtue is fairest in a poor array.

FORTUNE
Poor fool, 'tis not this badge of purity,
Nor Sibi sapit, painted on thy breast,
Allures mortality to seek thy love.
No: now the great wheel of thy globe hath run,
And met this first point of creation.
On crutches went this world but yesterday,
Now it lies bed-rid, and is grown so old,
That it's grown young; for 'tis a child again,
A childish soul it hath, 'tis a mere fool:
And fools and children are well pleased with toys.
So must this world, with shows it must be pleased,
Then, Virtue, buy a golden face like Vice,
And hang thy bosom full of silver moons,
To tell the credulous world, As those increase,
As the bright moon swells in her pearlèd sphere,
So wealth and pleasures them to Heaven shall rear.

VIRTUE
Virtue abhors to wear a borrowed face.

VICE
Why hast thou borrowed, then, that idiot's hood?

VIRTUE
Fools placed it on my head that knew me not,
And I am proud to wear the scorn of fools.

FORTUNE
Mourn in that pride and die, all the world hates thee.

VIRTUE
Not all, I'll wander once more through the world:
Wisdom I know hath with her blessèd wings
Fled to some bosom: if I meet that breast,
There I'll erect my temple, and there rest.
Fortune nor Vice shall then e'er have the power
By their loose eyes to entice my paramour.
Then will I cast off this deformity,
And shine in glory, and triumph to see
You conquered at my feet, that tread on me.

FORTUNE
Virtue begins to quarrel: Vice, farewell.

VICE
Stay, Fortune, whilst within this grove we dwell,
If my angelical and saint-like form
Can win some amorous fool to wanton here,
And taste the fruit of this alluring tree,
Thus shall his saucy brows adornèd be,
To make us laugh.

[Makes horns.

FORTUNE
It will be rare: adieu.

VIRTUE
Foul, hell-bred fiend, Virtue shall strive with you,
If any be enamoured of thine eyes,
Their love must needs beget deformities.
Men are transformed to beasts, feasting with sin;
But if in spite of thee their souls I win,
To taste this fruit, though thou disguise their head,
Their shapes shall be re-metamorphosèd.

VICE
I dare thee do thy worst.

VIRTUE

My best I'll try.

FORTUNATUS
Fortune shall judge who wins the sovereignty.

[Exeunt.

ACT THE SECOND

Enter CHORUS.

CHORUS.
The world to the circumference of Heaven
Is as a small point in geometry,
Whose greatness is so little, that a less
Cannot be made: into that narrow room,
Your quick imaginations we must charm,
To turn that world: and turned, again to part it
Into large kingdoms, and within one moment
To carry Fortunatus on the wings
Of active thought, many a thousand miles.
Suppose then, since you last beheld him here,
That you have sailed with him upon the seas,
And leapt with him upon the Asian shores,
Been feasted with him in the Tartar's palace,
And all the courts of each barbarian king:
From whence being called by some unlucky star,—
For happiness never continues long,
Help me to bring him back to Arragon,
Where for his pride—riches make all men proud—
On slight quarrel, by a covetous Earl,
Fortune's dear minion is imprisonèd.
There think you see him sit with folded arms,
Tears dropping down his cheeks, his white hairs torn,
His legs in rusty fetters, and his tongue
Bitterly cursing that his squint-eyed soul
Did not make choice of wisdom's sacred love.
Fortune, to triumph in inconstancy,
From prison bails him: liberty is wild,
For being set free, he like a lusty eagle
Cut with his vent'rous feathers through the sky,
And 'lights not till he find the Turkish court.
Thither transport your eyes, and there behold him,
Revelling with the Emperor of the East,
From whence through fear, for safeguard of his life,
Flying into the arms of ugly Night,

Suppose you see him brought to Babylon;
And that the sun clothed all in fire hath rid
One quarter of his hot celestial way
With the bright morning, and that in this instant,
He and the Soldan meet, but what they say,
Listen you—the talk of kings none dare bewray.

[Exit.

SCENE I.—The Court at Babylon.[36]

[36] In the original story Fortunatus goes to Cairo, and Dekker is evidently here confusing Egypt with Assyria. Hence the Soldan's court at Babylon.

Enter the SOLDAN, NOBLEMEN, and FORTUNATUS.

SOLDAN
Art thou that Fortunatus, whose great name,
Being carried in the chariot of the winds,
Hast filled the courts of all our Asian kings
With love and envy, whose dear presence ties
The eyes of admiration to thine eyes?
Art thou that Jove that in a shower of gold
Appeared'st before the Turkish Emperor?

FORTUNATUS
I am that Fortunatus, mighty Soldan.

SOLDAN
Where is that purse which threw abroad such treasure?

FORTUNATUS
I gave it to the Turkish Soliman,
A second I bestowed on Prester John,
A third the great Tartarian Cham received:
For with these monarchs have I banqueted,
And rid with them in triumph through their courts,
In crystal chariots drawn by unicorns.
England, France, Spain, and wealthy Belgia,
And all the rest of Europe's blessed daughters,
Have made my covetous eye rich in th' embrace
Of their celestial beauties; now I come
To see the glory of fair Babylon.
Is Fortunatus welcome to the Soldan?
For I am like the sun, if Jove once chide,
My gilded brows from amorous Heaven I hide.

SOLDAN
Most welcome, and most happy are mine arms
In circling such an earthly deity;
But will not Fortunatus make me blessed
By sight of such a purse?

FORTUNATUS
Ere I depart,
The Soldan shall receive one at my hands:
For I must spend some time in framing it,
And then some time to breathe that virtuous spirit
Into the heart thereof, all which is done
By a most sacred inspiration.

SOLDAN
Welcome, most welcome to the Soldan's court;
Stay here and be the King of Babylon:
Stay here, I will more amaze thine eyes
With wondrous sights, than can all Asia.
Behold yon town, there stands mine armoury,
In which are corselets forged of beaten gold,
To arm ten hundred thousand fighting men,
Whose glittering squadrons when the sun beholds,
They seem like to ten hundred thousand Joves,
When Jove on the proud back of thunder rides,
Trapped all in lightning flames: there can I show thee
The ball of gold that set all Troy on fire;[37]
There shalt thou see the scarf of Cupid's mother,
Snatched from the soft moist ivory of her arm,
To wrap about Adonis' wounded thigh;
There shalt thou see a wheel of Titan's care,
Which dropped from Heaven when Phaeton fired the world:[38]
I'll give thee, if thou wilt, two silver doves
Composed by magic to divide the air,
Who, as they fly, shall clap their silver wings,
And give strange music to the elements;
I'll give thee else the fan of Proserpine,
Which in reward for a sweet Thracian song,
The black-browed Empress threw to Orpheus,
Being come to fetch Eurydice from hell.

[37] *The golden apple which Paris adjudged to Venus.*

[38] *Alluding to Phaeton's flight, and the fiery disruption of his chariot.*

FORTUNATUS
Hath ever mortal eye beheld these wonders?

SOLDAN
Thine shall behold them, and make choice of any,
So thou wilt give the Soldan such a purse.

FORTUNATUS
By Fortune's blessèd hand, who christened me,
The mighty Soldan shall have such a purse,
Provided I may see these priceless wonders.

SOLDAN
Leave us alone: [Exeunt NOBLES.] never was mortal ear
Acquainted with the virtue of a jewel,
Which now I'll show, out-valuing all the rest.

FORTUNATUS
It is impossible.

SOLDAN
Behold this casket,

[Draws a curtain.

Fettered in golden chains, the lock pure gold,
The key of solid gold, which myself keep,
And here's the treasure that's contained in it.

[Takes out the hat.

FORTUNATUS
A coarse felt hat? is this the precious jewel?

SOLDAN
I'll not exchange this for ten diadems.
On pain of death, none listen to our talk.

FORTUNATUS
What needs this solemn conjuration!

SOLDAN
O, yes, for none shall understand the worth
Of this inestimable ornament,
But you: and yet not you, but that you swear
By her white hand, that lent you such a name,
To leave a wondrous purse in Babylon.

FORTUNATUS
What I have sworn, I will not violate,

But now uncover the virtues of this hat.

SOLDAN
I think none listen; if they do, they die.

FORTUNATUS
None listen: tell, what needs this jealousy?

SOLDAN
You see 'tis poor in show; did I want jewels,
Gold could beget them, but the wide world's wealth
Buys not this hat: this clapped upon my head,
I, only with a wish, am through the air
Transported in a moment over seas
And over lands to any secret place;
By this I steal to every prince's court,
And hear their private counsels and prevent
All dangers which to Babylon are meant;
By help of this I oft see armies join,
Though when the dreadful Alvarado[39] sounds,
I am distant from the place a thousand leagues.
Oh, had I such a purse and such a hat,
The Soldan were, of all, most fortunate.

[39] A martial term, probably of Spanish derivation, for the summons to battle.

FORTUNATUS
Oh, had I such a hat, then were I brave.
Where's he that made it?

SOLDAN
Dead, and the whole world
Yields not a workman that can frame the like.

FORTUNATUS
No, does't?[40] By what trick shall I make this mine?   [Aside.
Methinks, methinks, when you are borne o'er seas,
And over lands, the heaviness thereof
Should weigh you down, drown you, or break your neck.

[40] "No does?" simply in the original, which is not intelligible. In full it would seem to imply "No, does it not?"

SOLDAN
No, 'tis more light than any hat beside:
Your hand shall peise[41] it.

[41] Poise, weigh. "Peise" is still in use in some parts of the north of England.

FORTUNATUS
Oh, 'tis wondrous heavy.

SOLDAN
Fie, y'are deceived: try it upon your head.

FORTUNATUS
Would I were now in Cyprus with my sons.

[Exit.

SOLDAN
Stay! Fortunatus, stay! I am undone.
Treason, lords, treason, get me wings, I'll fly
After this damnèd traitor through the air.

Re-enter NOBLES.

NOBLES
Who wrongs the mighty King of Babylon?

SOLDAN
This Fortunatus, this fiend, wrongs your king.

NOBLES
Lock the court gates, where is the devil hid?

SOLDAN
No gates, no grates of iron imprison him,
Like a magician breaks he through the clouds,
Bearing my soul with him, for that jewel gone,
I am dead, and all is dross in Babylon.
Fly after him!—'tis vain: on the wind's wings,
He'll ride through all the courts of earthly kings.

NOBLES
What is the jewel that your grace hath lost?

SOLDAN
He dies that troubles me: call me not king;
For I'll consume my life in sorrowing.

[Exeunt.

SCENE II.—Outside the House of Fortunatus

Enter ANDELOCIA, very gallant,[42] and SHADOW.

[42] i.e. Gallantly attired.

ANDELOCIA
Shadow? what have I lost to-day at dice?

SHADOW
More than you will win again in a month.

ANDELOCIA
Why, sir, how much comes it to?

SHADOW
It comes to nothing, sir, for you have lost your wits; and when a man's wits are lost, the man is like twenty pounds' worth of tobacco, which mounts into th' air, and proves nothing but one thing.

ANDELOCIA
And what thing is that, you ass?

SHADOW
Marry, sir, that he is an ass that melts so much money in smoke.

ANDELOCIA
'Twere a charitable deed to hang thee a smoking.

SHADOW
I should never make good bacon, because I am not fat.

ANDELOCIA
I'll be sworn thy wit is lean.

SHADOW
It's happy I have a lean wit: but, master, you have none; for when your money tripped away, that went after it, and ever since you have been mad. Here comes your brother.

Enter AMPEDO.

Borrow a dram of him, if his be not mouldy: for men's wits in these days are like the cuckoo, bald once a year, and that makes motley so dear, and fools so good cheap.

ANDELOCIA
Brother, all hail.

SHADOW
There's a rattling salutation.

ANDELOCIA
You must lend me some more money. Nay, never look so strange, an you will come off, so; if you will bar me from square play, do. Come, come, when the old traveller my father comes home, like a young ape, full of fantastic tricks, or a painted parrot stuck full of outlandish feathers, he'll lead the world in a string, and then like a hot shot I'll charge and discharge all.

SHADOW
I would be loth, master, to see that day: for he leads the world in a string that goes to hanging.

ANDELOCIA
Take heed I turn not that head into the world, and lead you so.
Brother wilt be? Ha' ye any ends of gold or silver?

AMPEDO
Thus wanton revelling breeds beggary.
Brother, 'twere better that you still lived poor.
Want would make wisdom rich: but when your coffers
Swell to the brim, then riot sets up sails,
And like a desperate unskilled mariner
Drives your unsteady fortunes on the point
Of wreck inevitable. Of all the wealth
Left by our father, when he left us last,
This little is unspent, and this being wasted,
Your riot ends; therefore consume it all.
I'll live; or dying, find some burial.

ANDELOCIA
Thanks for my crowns.[43] Shadow, I am villainous hungry, to hear one of the seven wise masters talk thus emptily.

[43] *In the original these words are assigned to Ampedo, an evident error.*

SHADOW
I am a villain, master, if I am not hungry.

ANDELOCIA
Because I'll save this gold, sirrah Shadow, we'll feed ourselves with paradoxes.

SHADOW
Oh rare: what meat's that?

ANDELOCIA
Meat, you gull: 'tis no meat: a dish of paradoxes is a feast of strange opinion, 'tis an ordinary that our greatest gallants haunt nowadays, because they would be held for statesmen.

SHADOW
I shall never fill my belly with opinions.

ANDELOCIA
In despite of sway-bellies, gluttons, and sweet mouthed epicures, I'll have thee maintain a paradox in commendations of hunger.

SHADOW
I shall never have the stomach to do't.

ANDELOCIA
See'st thou this crusado?[44] do it, and turn this into a feast.

[44] *A Portuguese coin having a cross on one side and worth about 2s. 3d., but varying in value at different times.*

SHADOW
Covetousness and lechery are two devils, they'll tempt a man to wade through deep matters: I'll do't though good cheer conspire my death, for speaking treason against her.

ANDELOCIA
Fall to it then with a full mouth.

SHADOW
Oh famine, inspire me with thy miserable reasons.
I begin, master.

AMPEDO
O miserable invocation.

ANDELOCIA
Silence!

SHADOW
There's no man but loves one of these three beasts, a horse, a hound, or a whore; the horse by his goodwill has his head ever in the manger; the whore with your ill will has her hand ever in your purse; and a hungry dog eats dirty puddings.

ANDELOCIA
This is profound, forward: the conclusion of this now.

SHADOW
The conclusion is plain: for since all men love one of these three monsters, being such terrible eaters, therefore all men love hunger.

AMPEDO
A very lean argument.

SHADOW
I can make it no fatter.

ANDELOCIA
Proceed, good Shadow; this fats me.

SHADOW
Hunger is made of gunpowder.

ANDELOCIA
Give fire to that opinion.

SHADOW
Stand by, lest it blow you up. Hunger is made of gunpowder, or gunpowder of hunger, for they both eat through stone walls; hunger is a grindstone, it sharpens wit; hunger is fuller of love than Cupid, for it makes a man eat himself; hunger was the first that ever opened a cook shop, cooks the first that ever made sauce, sauce being liquorish, licks up good meat; good meat preserves life: hunger therefore preserves life.

AMPEDO
By my consent thou shouldst still live by hunger.

SHADOW
Not so, hunger makes no man mortal: hunger is an excellent physician, for he dares kill any body. Hunger is one of the seven liberal sciences.

ANDELOCIA
Oh learned! Which of the seven?

SHADOW
Music, for she'll make a man leap at a crust; but as few care for her six sisters, so none love to dance after her pipe. Hunger, master, is hungry and covetous; therefore the crusado.

ANDELOCIA
But hast thou no sharper reasons than this?

SHADOW
Yes, one: the dagger of Cyprus had never stabbed out such six penny pipes, but for hunger.

ANDELOCIA
Why, you dolt, these pipes are but in their minority.

SHADOW
My belly and my purse have been twenty times at dagger's drawing, with parting the little urchins.

Enter FORTUNATUS.

AMPEDO
Peace, idiot, peace, my father is returned.

FORTUNATUS
Touch me not, boys, I am nothing but air; let none speak to me, till you have marked me well.

SHADOW (Chalking FORTUNATUS' back.)
Now speak your mind.

AMPEDO
Villain, why hast thou chalked my father's back?

SHADOW
Only to mark him, and to try what colour air is of.

FORTUNATUS
Regard him not, Ampedo: Andelocia, Shadow, view me, am I as you are, or am I transformed?

ANDELOCIA
I thought travel would turn my father madman or fool.

AMPEDO
How should you be transformed? I see no change.

SHADOW
If your wits be not planet stricken, if your brains lie in their right place, you are well enough; for your body is little mended by your fetching vagaries.

ANDELOCIA
Methinks, father, you look as you did, only your face is more withered.

FORTUNATUS
That's not my fault; age is like love, it cannot be hid.

SHADOW
Or like gunpowder a-fire, or like a fool, or like a young novice new come to his lands: for all these will show of what house they come. Now, sir, you may amplify.

FORTUNATUS
Shadow, turn thy tongue to a shadow, be silent! Boys, be proud, your father hath the whole world in this compass, I am all felicity, up to the brims. In a minute am I come from Babylon, I have been this half-hour in Famagosta.

ANDELOCIA
How? in a minute, father? Ha, ha, I see travellers must lie.

SHADOW
'Tis their destiny: the Fates do so conspire.

FORTUNATUS
I have cut through the air like a falcon; I would have it seem strange to you.

SHADOW
So it does, sir.

FORTUNATUS
But 'tis true: I would not have you believe it neither.

SHADOW
No more we do not, sir.

FORTUNATUS
But 'tis miraculous and true. Desire to see you, brought me to Cyprus. I'll leave you more gold, and go visit more countries.

SHADOW
Leave us gold enough, and we'll make all countries come visit us.

AMPEDO
The frosty hand of age now nips your blood,
And strews her snowy flowers upon your head,
And gives you warning that within few years,
Death needs must marry you: those short-lived minutes,
That dribble out your life, must needs be spent
In peace, not travel: rest in Cyprus then.
Could you survey ten worlds, yet you must die;
And bitter is the sweet that's reaped thereby.

ANDELOCIA
Faith, father, what pleasure have you met by walking your stations?

FORTUNATUS
What pleasure, boy? I have revelled with kings, danced with queens, dallied with ladies, worn strange attires, seen fantasticos, conversed with humorists, been ravished with divine raptures of Doric, Lydian and Phrygian harmonies. I have spent the day in triumphs, and the night in banqueting.

ANDELOCIA
Oh rare: this was heavenly.

SHADOW
Methinks 'twas horrible.

ANDELOCIA
He that would not be an Arabian phœnix to burn in these sweet fires, let him live like an owl for the world to wonder at.

AMPEDO
Why, brother, are not all these vanities?

FORTUNATUS
Vanities? Ampedo, thy soul is made of lead, too dull, too ponderous to mount up to the incomprehensible glory that travel lifts men to.

SHADOW
My old master's soul is cork and feathers, and being so light doth easily mount up.

ANDELOCIA
Sweeten mine ears, good father, with some more.

FORTUNATUS
When in the warmth of mine own country's arms
We yawned like sluggards, when this small horizon
Imprisoned up my body, then mine eyes
Worshipped these clouds as brightest; but, my boys,
The glist'ring beams which do abroad appear
In other heavens,—fire is not half so clear.

SHADOW
Why, sir, are there other heavens in other countries?

ANDELOCIA
Peace; interrupt him not upon thy life.

FORTUNATUS
For still in all the regions I have seen,
I scorned to crowd among the muddy throng
Of the rank multitude, whose thickened breath,
Like to condensèd fogs, do choke that beauty,
Which else would dwell in every kingdom's cheek.
No, I still boldly stept into their courts,
For there to live 'tis rare, O 'tis divine;
There shall you see faces angelical,
There shall you see troops of chaste goddesses,
Whose star-like eyes have power, might they still shine,
To make night day, and day more crystalline.
Near these you shall behold great heroes,
White-headed counsellors and jovial spirits,
Standing like fiery cherubims to guard
The monarch, who in god-like glory sits
In midst of these, as if this deity
Had with a look created a new world,
The standers by being the fair workmanship.

ANDELOCIA
Oh how my soul is rapt to a third heaven. I'll travel sure, and live with none but kings.

SHADOW

Then Shadow must die among knaves; and yet why so? In a bunch of cards, knaves wait upon the kings.

ANDELOCIA
When I turn king, then shalt thou wait on me.

SHADOW
Well, there's nothing impossible: a dog has his day, and so have you.

AMPEDO
But tell me, father, have you in all courts
Beheld such glory, so majestical
In all perfection, no way blemishèd?

FORTUNATUS
In some courts shall you see ambition
Sit piercing Dedalus' old waxen wings,
But being clapped on, and they about to fly,
Even when their hopes are busied in the clouds,
They melt against the sun of majesty,
And down they tumble to destruction:
For since the Heaven's strong arms teach kings to stand,
Angels are placed about their glorious throne,
To guard it from the strokes of trait'rous hands.
By travel, boys, I have seen all these things.
Fantastic compliment stalks up and down,
Tricked in outlandish feathers, all his words,
His looks, his oaths, are all ridiculous,
All apish, childish, and Italianate.[45]

[45] *A common reproach for the affectation of the courtiers in Elizabeth's reign.*

Enter FORTUNE in the background: after her The Three Destinies,[46] working.

[46] *"The Parcae were generally represented as three old women with chaplets made with wool, and interwoven with the flowers of the narcissus. They were covered with a white robe, and fillet of the same colour, bound with chaplets. One of them held a distaff, another the spindle, and the third was armed with scissors with which she cut the thread which her sisters had spun."—Lempriere.*

SHADOW
I know a medicine for that malady.

FORTUNATUS
By travel, boys, I have seen all these things.

ANDELOCIA
And these are sights for none but gods and kings.

SHADOW

Yes, and for Christian creatures, if they be not blind.

FORTUNATUS
In these two hands do I grip all the world.
This leather purse, and this bald woollen hat
Make me a monarch. Here's my crown and sceptre!
In progress will I now go through the world.
I'll crack your shoulders, boys, with bags of gold
Ere I depart; on Fortune's wings I ride,
And now sit in the height of human pride.

FORTUNE
(Coming forward.) Now, fool, thou liest; where thy proud feet do tread,
These shall throw down thy cold and breathless head.

FORTUNATUS
O sacred deity, what sin is done,
That Death's iron fist should wrestle with thy son?

[All kneel.

FORTUNE
Thou art no son of Fortune, but her slave:
Thy cedar hath aspired to his full height.
Thy sun-like glory hath advanced herself
Into the top of pride's meridian,
And down amain it comes. From beggary
I plumed thee like an ostrich, like that ostrich
Thou hast eaten metals, and abused my gifts,
Hast played the ruffian, wasted that in riots
Which as a blessing I bestowed on thee.

FORTUNATUS
Forgive me, I will be more provident.

FORTUNE
No, endless follies follow endless wealth.
Thou hadst thy fancy, I must have thy fate,
Which is, to die when th'art most fortunate.
This inky thread, thy ugly sins have spun,
Black life, black death; faster! that it were done.

FORTUNATUS
Oh, let me live, but till I can redeem.

FORTUNE
The Destinies deny thee longer life.

FORTUNATUS
I am but now lifted to happiness.

FORTUNE
And now I take most pride to cast thee down.
Hadst thou chosen wisdom, this black had been white,
And Death's stern brow could not thy soul affright.

FORTUNATUS
Take this again! (Offering the purse.) Give wisdom to my sons.

FORTUNE
No, fool, 'tis now too late: as death strikes thee,
So shall their ends sudden and wretched be.
Jove's daughters—righteous Destinies—make haste!
His life hath wasteful been, and let it waste.

[Exeunt FORTUNE and The Three Destinies.

ANDELOCIA
Why the pox dost thou sweat so?

SHADOW
For anger to see any of God's creatures have such filthy
faces as these sempsters[47] had that went hence.

[47] Sempstresses, alluding to their spinning.

ANDELOCIA
Sempsters? why, you ass, they are Destinies.

SHADOW
Indeed, if it be one's destiny to have a filthy face, I know no remedy but to go masked and cry "Woe worth the Fates."

AMPEDO
Why droops my father? these are only shadows,
Raised by the malice of some enemy,
To fright your life, o'er which they have no power.

SHADOW
Shadows? I defy their kindred.

FORTUNATUS
O Ampedo, I faint; help me, my sons.

ANDELOCIA
Shadow, I pray thee run and call more help.

SHADOW
If that desperate Don Dego[48] Death hath ta'en up the cudgels once, here's never a fencer in Cyprus dare take my old master's part.

[48] See The Devil's Answer to Pierce Pennylesse, p. 100, "that great Dego of Devils."—Dekker's Non-Dramatic Works.

ANDELOCIA
Run, villain, call more help.

SHADOW
Bid him thank the Destinies for this.

[Exit.

FORTUNATUS
Let me shrink down, and die between your arms,
Help comes in vain. No hand can conquer fate,
This instant is the last of my life's date.
This goddess, if at least she be a goddess,
Names herself Fortune: wand'ring in a wood,
Half famished, her I met. I have, quoth she,
Six gifts to spend upon mortality,
Wisdom, strength, health, beauty, long life and riches.
Out of my bounty one of these is thine.

AMPEDO
What benefit did from your choice arise?

FORTUNATUS
Listen, my sons! in this small compass lies
Infinite treasure: this she gave to me,
And gave to this, this virtue, Take, quoth she,
So often as from hence thou draw'st thy hand,
Ten golden pieces of that kingdom's coin,
Where'er thou liv'st; which plenteous sure shall last,
After thy death, till thy sons' lives do waste.

ANDELOCIA
Father, your choice was rare, the gift divine.

FORTUNATUS
It had been so, if riches had been mine.

AMPEDO
But hath this golden virtue never failed?

FORTUNATUS
Never.

ANDELOCIA
O admirable: here's a fire
Hath power to thaw the very heart of death,
And give stones life; by this most sacred breath,
See brother, here's all India in my hand.

FORTUNATUS
Inherit you, my sons, that golden land.
This hat I brought away from Babylon,
I robbed the Soldan of it, 'tis a prize
Worth twenty empires in this jewel lies.

ANDELOCIA
How, father? jewel? call you this a jewel? it's coarse wool, a bald fashion, and greasy to the brim; I have bought a better felt for a French crown forty times: of what virtuous block is this hat, I pray?

FORTUNATUS
Set it upon thy head, and wish a wish,
Thou in the moment, on the wind's swift wings,
Shalt be transported into any place.

ANDELOCIA
A wishing hat, and a golden mine?

FORTUNATUS
O Andelocia, Ampedo, now Death
Sounds his third summons, I must hence! These jewels
To both I do bequeath; divide them not,
But use them equally: never bewray
What virtues are in them; for if you do,
Much shame, much grief, much danger follows you.
Peruse this book; farewell! behold in me
The rotten strength of proud mortality.

[Dies.

AMPEDO
His soul is wandering to the Elysian shades.

ANDELOCIA
The flower that's fresh at noon, at sunset fades.
Brother, close you down his eyes, because you were his eldest; and with them close up your tears, whilst I as all younger brothers do, shift for myself: let us mourn, because he's dead, but mourn the less, because he cannot revive. The honour we can do him, is to bury him royally; let's about it then, for I'll

not melt myself to death with scalding sighs, nor drop my soul out at mine eyes, were my father an emperor.

AMPEDO
Hence, hence, thou stop'st the tide of my true tears.
True grief is dumb, though it hath open ears.

ANDELOCIA
Yet God send my grief a tongue, that I may have good utterance for it: sob on, brother mine, whilst you sigh there, I'll sit and read what story my father has written here.

[They both fall asleep: FORTUNE and a company of Satyrs enter with music, and playing about FORTUNATUS' body, take it away. Afterwards SHADOW enters running.

SHADOW
I can get none, I can find none: where are you, master? Have I ta'en you napping? and you too? I see sorrow's eye-lids are made of a dormouse skin, they seldom open, or of a miser's purse, that's always shut. So ho, master.

ANDELOCIA
Shadow, why how now? what's the matter?

SHADOW
I can get none, sir, 'tis impossible.

AMPEDO
What is impossible? what canst not get?

SHADOW
No help for my old master.

ANDELOCIA
Hast thou been all this while calling for help?

SHADOW
Yes, sir: he scorned all Famagosta when he was in his huffing,[49] and now he lies puffing for wind, they say they scorn him.

[49] Swaggering mood.

AMPEDO
The poison of their scorn infects not him;
He wants no help. See where he breathless lies:
Brother, to what place have you borne his body?

ANDELOCIA
I bear it? I touched it not.

AMPEDO
Nor I: a leaden slumber pressed mine eyes.

SHADOW
Whether it were lead or latten[50] that hasped down those winking casements, I know not, but I found you both snorting.

[50] Ital. Latta, tin-plate.

AMPEDO
And in that sleep, methought, I heard the tunes
Of sullen passions apt for funerals,
And saw my father's lifeless body borne
By Satyrs: O I fear that deity
Hath stolen him hence!—that snudge, his destiny.

ANDELOCIA
I fear he's risen again; didst not thou meet him?

SHADOW
I, sir? do you think this white and red durst have kissed my sweet cheeks, if they had seen a ghost? But, master, if the Destinies, or Fortune, or the Fates, or the Fairies have stolen him, never indict them for the felony: for by this means the charges of a tomb is saved, and you being his heirs, may do as many rich executors do, put that money in your purses, and give out that he died a beggar.

ANDELOCIA
Away, you rogue, my father die a beggar!
I'll build a tomb for him of massy gold.

SHADOW
Methinks, master, it were better to let the memory of him shine in his own virtues, if he had any, than in alabaster.

ANDELOCIA
I shall mangle that alabaster face, you whoreson virtuous vice.

SHADOW
He has a marble heart, that can mangle a face of alabaster.

ANDELOCIA
Brother, come, come, mourn not; our father is but stepped to agree with Charon for his boat hire to Elysium. See, here's a story of all his travels; this book shall come out with a new addition: I'll tread after my father's steps; I'll go measure the world, therefore let's share these jewels, take this, or this!

AMPEDO
Will you then violate our father's will?

ANDELOCIA

A Puritan!—keep a dead man's will? Indeed in the old time, when men were buried in soft church-yards, that their ghosts might rise, it was good: but, brother, now they are imprisoned in strong brick and marble, they are fast. Fear not: away, away, these are fooleries, gulleries, trumperies; here's this or this, or I am gone with both!

AMPEDO
Do you as you please, the sin shall not be mine. Fools call those things profane that are divine.

ANDELOCIA
Are you content to wear the jewels by turns? I'll have the purse for a year, you the hat, and as much gold as you'll ask; and when my pursership ends, I'll resign, and cap you.

AMPEDO
I am content to bear all discontents.

[Exit.

ANDELOCIA
I should serve this bearing ass rarely now, if I should load him, but I will not. Though conscience be like physic, seldom used, for so it does least hurt, yet I'll take a dram of it. This for him, and some gold: this for me; for having this mint about me, I shall want no wishing cap. Gold is an eagle, that can fly to any place, and, like death, that dares enter all places. Shadow, wilt thou travel with me?

SHADOW
I shall never fadge[382] with the humour because I cannot lie.

[382] Succeed.

ANDELOCIA
Thou dolt, we'll visit all the kings' courts in the world.

SHADOW
So we may, and return dolts home, but what shall we learn by travel?

ANDELOCIA
Fashions.[51]

[51] Farcy, a disease to which horses are subject, still sometimes miscalled "Fashions" by country farriers. Dekker puns on it again in The Gull's Horn-Book:—"Fashions then was counted a disease, and horses died of it: But now (thanks to folly) it is held the only rare physic, and the purest golden Asses live upon it."

SHADOW
That's a beastly disease: methinks it's better staying in your own country.

ANDELOCIA
How? In mine own country—like a cage-bird, and see nothing?

SHADOW
Nothing? yes, you may see things enough, for what can you see abroad that is not at home? The same sun calls you up in the morning, and the same man in the moon lights you to bed at night; our fields are as green as theirs in summer, and their frosts will nip us more in winter: our birds sing as sweetly and our women are as fair: in other countries you shall have one drink to you; whilst you kiss your hand, and duck,[52] he'll poison you: I confess you shall meet more fools, and asses, and knaves abroad than at home. Yet God be thanked we have pretty store of all. But for punks,[53] we put them down.

[52] Bow.

[53] Prostitutes.

ANDELOCIA
Prepare thy spirits, for thou shalt go with me.
To England shall our stars direct our course;
Thither the Prince of Cyprus, our king's son,
Is gone to see the lovely Agripyne.
Shadow, we'll gaze upon that English dame,
And try what virtue gold has to inflame.
First to my brother, then away let's fly;
Shadow must be a courtier ere he die.

[Exit.

SHADOW
If I must, the Fates shall be served: I have seen many clowns courtiers, then why not Shadow? Fortune, I am for thee.

[Exit.

ACT THE THIRD.

SCENE I.—London. The Court of Athelstane

Enter ORLEANS melancholy, GALLOWAY with him; a BOY after them with a lute.

ORLEANS
Begone: leave that with me, and leave me to myself; if the king ask for me, swear to him I am sick, and thou shalt not lie; pray thee leave me.

BOY
I am gone, sir.

[Exit.

ORLEANS
This music makes me but more out of tune.
O, Agripyne.

GALLOWAY
Gentle friend, no more.
Thou sayest love is a madness, hate it then,
Even for the name's sake.

ORLEANS
O, I love that madness,
Even for the name's sake.

GALLOWAY
Let me tame this frenzy,
By telling thee thou art a prisoner here,
By telling thee she's daughter to a king,
By telling thee the King of Cyprus' son
Shines like a sun, between her looks and thine,
Whilst thou seem'st but a star to Agripyne:
He loves her.

ORLEANS
If he do: why so do I.

GALLOWAY
Love is ambitious, and loves majesty.

ORLEANS
Dear friend, thou art deceived, love's voice doth sing
As sweetly in a beggar as a king.

GALLOWAY
Dear friend, thou art deceived: O bid thy soul
Lift up her intellectual eyes to Heaven,
And in this ample book of wonders read,
Of what celestial mould, what sacred essence,
Herself is formed, the search whereof will drive
Sounds musical among the jarring spirits,
And in sweet tune set that which none inherits.

ORLEANS
I'll gaze on Heaven if Agripyne be there:
If not: fa, la, la, sol, la, &c.

GALLOWAY
O, call this madness in; see, from the windows
Of every eye derision thrusts out cheeks,

Wrinkled with idiot laughter; every finger
Is like a dart shot from the hand of scorn,
By which thy name is hurt, thine honour torn.

ORLEANS
Laugh they at me, sweet Galloway?

GALLOWAY
Even at thee.

ORLEANS
Ha, ha, I laugh at them, are not they mad
That let my true true sorrow make them glad?
I dance and sing only to anger grief,
That in that anger, he might smite life down
With his iron fist. Good heart, it seemeth then,
They laugh to see grief kill me: O, fond men,
You laugh at others' tears; when others smile,
You tear yourselves in pieces: vile, vile, vile!
Ha, ha, when I behold a swarm of fools,
Crowding together to be counted wise,
I laugh because sweet Agripyne's not there,
But weep because she is not anywhere,
And weep because whether she be or not,
My love was ever, and is still, forgot: forgot, forgot, forgot.

GALLOWAY
Draw back this stream, why should my Orleans mourn?

ORLEANS
Look yonder, Galloway, dost thou see that sun?
Nay, good friend, stare upon it, mark it well,
Ere he be two hours older, all that glory
Is banished Heaven, and then for grief this sky,
That's now so jocund, will mourn all in black,
And shall not Orleans mourn? Alack, alack!
O what a savage tyranny it were
T'enforce care laugh, and woe not shed a tear!
Dead is my love, I am buried in her scorn,
That is my sunset, and shall I not mourn?
Yes, by my troth I will.

GALLOWAY
Dear friend, forbear,
Beauty, like sorrow, dwelleth everywhere.
Rase out this strong idea of her face,
As fair as hers shineth in any place.

ORLEANS
Thou art a traitor to that white and red,
Which, sitting on her cheeks, being Cupid's throne,
Is my heart's sovereign: O, when she is dead,
This wonder, beauty, shall be found in none.
Now Agripyne's not mine, I vow to be
In love with nothing but deformity.
O fair Deformity, I muse all eyes
Are not enamoured of thee: thou didst never
Murder men's hearts, or let them pine like wax,
Melting against the sun of destiny;
Thou art a faithful nurse to chastity;
Thy beauty is not like to Agripyne's,
For cares, and age, and sickness hers deface,
But thine's eternal. O Deformity,
Thy fairness is not like to Agripyne's,
For dead, her beauty will no beauty have,
But thy face looks most lovely in the grave.

Enter the PRINCE OF CYPRUS and AGRIPYNE.

GALLOWAY
See where they come together, hand in hand.

ORLEANS
O watch, sweet Galloway, when their hands do part,
Between them shalt thou find my murdered heart.

CYPRUS
By this then it seems a thing impossible, to know when an English lady loves truly.

AGRIPYNE
Not so, for when her soul steals into her heart, and her heart leaps up to her eyes, and her eyes drop into her hands, then if she say, Here's my hand! she's your own,—else never.

CYPRUS
Here's a pair of your prisoners, let's try their opinion.

AGRIPYNE
My kind prisoners, well encountered; the Prince of Cyprus here and myself have been wrangling about a question of love: my lord of Orleans, you look lean, and likest a lover—Whether is it more torment to love a lady and never enjoy her, or always to enjoy a lady whom you cannot choose but hate?

ORLEANS
To hold her ever in mine arms whom I loath in my heart, were some plague, yet the punishment were no more than to be enjoined to keep poison in my hand, yet never to taste it.

AGRIPYNE

But say you should be compelled to swallow the poison?

ORLEANS
Then a speedy death would end a speeding misery. But to love a lady and never enjoy her, oh it is not death, but worse than damnation; 'tis hell, 'tis—

AGRIPYNE
No more, no more, good Orleans; nay then, I see my prisoner is in love too.

CYPRUS
Methinks, soldiers cannot fall into the fashion of love.

AGRIPYNE
Methinks a soldier is the most faithful lover of all men else; for his affection stands not upon compliment. His wooing is plain home-spun stuff; there's no outlandish thread in it, no rhetoric. A soldier casts no figures to get his mistress' heart; his love is like his valour in the field, when he pays downright blows.

GALLOWAY
True, madam, but would you receive such payment?

AGRIPYNE
No, but I mean, I love a soldier best for his plain dealing.

CYPRUS
That's as good as the first.

AGRIPYNE
Be it so, that goodness I like: for what lady can abide to love a spruce silken-face courtier, that stands every morning two or three hours learning how to look by his glass, how to speak by his glass, how to sigh by his glass, how to court his mistress by his glass? I would wish him no other plague, but to have a mistress as brittle as glass.

GALLOWAY
And that were as bad as the horn plague.

CYPRUS
Are any lovers possessed with this madness?

AGRIPYNE
What madmen are not possessed with this love? Yet by my troth, we poor women do but smile in our sleeves to see all this foppery: yet we all desire to see our lovers attired gallantly, to hear them sing sweetly, to behold them dance comely and such like. But this apish monkey fashion of effeminate niceness, out upon it! Oh, I hate it worse than to be counted a scold.

CYPRUS
Indeed, men are most regarded, when they least regard themselves.

GALLOWAY
And women most honoured, when they show most mercy to their lovers.

ORLEANS
But is't not a miserable tyranny, to see a lady triumph in the passions of a soul languishing through her cruelty?

CYPRUS
Methinks it is.

GALLOWAY
Methinks 'tis more than tyranny.

AGRIPYNE
So think not I; for as there is no reason to hate any that love us, so it were madness to love all that do not hate us; women are created beautiful, only because men should woo them; for 'twere miserable tyranny to enjoin poor women to woo men: I would not hear of a woman in love, for my father's kingdom.

CYPRUS
I never heard of any woman that hated love.

AGRIPYNE
Nor I: but we had all rather die than confess we love; our glory is to hear men sigh whilst we smile, to kill them with a frown, to strike them dead with a sharp eye, to make you this day wear a feather, and to-morrow a sick nightcap. Oh, why this is rare, there's a certain deity in this, when a lady by the magic of her looks, can turn a man into twenty shapes.

ORLEANS
Sweet friend, she speaks this but to torture me.

GALLOWAY
I'll teach thee how to plague her: love her not.

AGRIPYNE
Poor Orleans, how lamentably he looks: if he stay, he'll make me surely love him for pure pity. I must send him hence, for of all sorts of love, I hate the French; I pray thee, sweet prisoner, entreat Lord Longaville to come to me presently.

ORLEANS
I will, and esteem myself more than happy, that you will employ me.

[Exit.

AGRIPYNE
Watch him, watch him for God's sake, if he sigh not or look not back.

CYPRUS

He does both: but what mystery lies in this?

AGRIPYNE
Nay, no mystery, 'tis as plain as Cupid's forehead: why this is as it should be.—"And esteem myself more than happy, that you will employ me." My French prisoner is in love over head and ears.

CYPRUS
It's wonder how he 'scapes drowning.

GALLOWAY
With whom, think you?

AGRIPYNE
With his keeper, for a good wager: Ah, how glad is he to obey! And how proud am I to command in this empire of affection! Over him and such spongy-livered youths, that lie soaking in love, I triumph more with mine eye, than ever he did over a soldier with his sword. Is't not a gallant victory for me to subdue my father's enemy with a look? Prince of Cyprus, you were best take heed, how you encounter an English lady.

CYPRUS
God bless me from loving any of you, if all be so cruel.

AGRIPYNE
God bless me from suffering you to love me, if you be not so formable.

CYPRUS
Will you command me any service, as you have done Orleans?

AGRIPYNE
No other service but this, that, as Orleans, you love me, for no other reason, but that I may torment you.

CYPRUS
I will: conditionally, that in all company I may call you my tormentor.

AGRIPYNE
You shall: conditionally, that you never beg for mercy.
Come, my Lord of Galloway.

GALLOWAY
Come, sweet madam.

[Exeunt all except the PRINCE OF CYPRUS.

CYPRUS
The ruby-coloured portals of her speech
Were closed by mercy: but upon her eye,
Attired in frowns, sat murdering cruelty.

Re-enter AGRIPYNE and listens.

She's angry, that I durst so high aspire.
O, she disdains that any stranger's breast
Should be a temple for her deity:
She's full of beauty, full of bitterness.
Till now, I did not dally with love's fire:
And when I thought to try his flames indeed,
I burnt me even to cinders. O, my stars,
Why from my native shore did your beams guide me,
To make me dote on her that doth deride me?

[AGRIPYNE kneels: CYPRUS walks musing.

AGRIPYNE
Hold him in this mind, sweet Cupid, I conjure thee. O, what music these hey-hos make! I was about to cast my little self into a great love trance for him, fearing his heart had been flint: but since I see 'tis pure virgin wax, he shall melt his bellyful: for now I know how to temper him.

[Exit; as she departs CYPRUS spies her.

CYPRUS
Never beg mercy? yet be my tormentor.
I hope she heard me not: doubtless she did,
And now will she insult upon my passions,
And vex my constant love with mockeries.
Nay, then I'll be mine own physician,
And outface love, and make her think that I
Mourned thus, because I saw her standing by.
What news, my Lord of Cornwall?

Enter CORNWALL.

CORNWALL
This fair prince,
One of your countrymen, is come to court,
A lusty gallant brave, in Cyprus' isle,
With fifty bard[54] horses prancing at his heels,
Backed by as many strong-limbed Cypriots,
All whom he keeps in pay: whose offered service,
Our king with arms of gladness hath embraced.

[54] Barded, or barbed: i.e. Adorned with trappings.

CYPRUS
Born in the isle of Cyprus? what's his name?

CORNWALL

His servants call him Fortunatus' son.

CYPRUS
Rich Fortunatus' son? Is he arrived?

Enter LONGAVILLE, GALLOWAY, and CHESTER with jewels.

LONGAVILLE
This he bestowed on me.

CHESTER
And this on me.

GALLOWAY
And this his bounteous hand enforced me take.

LONGAVILLE
I prize this jewel at a hundred marks,[55]
Yet would he needs bestow this gift on me.

[55] *The mark was worth 13s. 4d.*

CYPRUS
My lords, whose hand hath been thus prodigal?

GALLOWAY
Your countryman, my lord, a Cypriot.

LONGAVILLE
The gallant sure is all compact of gold,
To every lady hath he given rich jewels,
And sent to every servant in the court
Twenty fair English angels.[56]

[56] *The angel varied from 6s. 8d. to 10s. in value.*

CYPRUS
This is rare.

Enter LINCOLN.

LINCOLN
My lords, prepare yourselves for revelling,
'Tis the king's pleasure that this day be spent
In royal pastimes, that this golden lord,
For so all that behold him, christen him,
May taste the pleasures of our English court.
Here comes the gallant, shining like the sun.

[Trumpets sound.

Enter ATHELSTANE, ANDELOCIA, AGRIPYNE, ORLEANS, Ladies, and other Attendants, also INSULTADO. Music sounds within.

ANDELOCIA
For these your royal favours done to me,
Being a poor stranger, my best powers shall prove,
By acts of worth, the soundness of my love.

ATHELSTANE
Herein your love shall best set out itself,
By staying with us: if our English isle
Hold any object welcome to your eyes,
Do but make choice, and claim it as your prize.

[The KING and CYPRUS confer aside.

ANDELOCIA
I thank your grace: would he durst keep his word,
I know what I would claim. Tush, man, be bold,
Were she a saint, she may be won with gold.

CYPRUS
'Tis strange, I must confess, but in this pride,
His father Fortunatus, if he live,
Consumes his life in Cyprus: still he spends,
And still his coffers with abundance swell,
But how he gets these riches none can tell.

[The KING and AGRIPYNE confer aside.

ATHELSTANE
Hold him in talk: come hither, Agripyne.

CYPRUS
But what enticed young Andelocia's soul
To wander hither?

ANDELOCIA
That which did allure
My sovereign's son, the wonder of the place.

AGRIPYNE
This curious heap of wonders, which an Empress
Gave him, he gave me, and by Venus' hand,
The warlike Amorato needs would swear,

He left his country Cyprus for my love.

ATHELSTANE
If by the sovereign magic of thine eye,
Thou canst enchant his looks to keep the circles
Of thy fair cheeks, be bold to try their charms,
Feed him with hopes, and find the royal vein,
That leads this Cypriot to his golden mine.
Here's music spent in vain, lords, fall to dancing.

CYPRUS
My fair tormentor, will you lend a hand?

AGRIPYNE
I'll try this stranger's cunning[57] in a dance.

[57] Skill.

ANDELOCIA
My cunning is but small, yet who'll not prove
To shame himself for such a lady's love?

ORLEANS
These Cypriots are the devils that torture me.
He courts her, and she smiles, but I am born
To be her beauty's slave, and her love's scorn.

ANDELOCIA
I shall never have the face to ask the question twice.

AGRIPYNE
What's the reason? Cowardliness or pride?

ANDELOCIA
Neither: but 'tis the fashion of us Cypriots, both men and women, to yield at first assault, and we expect others should do the like.

AGRIPYNE
It's a sign, that either your women are very black, and are glad to be sped, or your men very fond, and will take no denial.

ANDELOCIA
Indeed our ladies are not so fair as you.

AGRIPYNE
But your men more venturous at a breach than you, or else they are all dastardly soldiers.

ANDELOCIA

He that fights under these sweet colours, and yet turns coward, let him be shot to death with the terrible arrows of fair ladies' eyes.

ATHELSTANE
Nay, Insultado, you must not deny us.

INSULTAD
Mi corazon es muy pesado, mi anima muy atormentada.
No por los Cielos: El pie de Español no hace musica en tierra ingles.[58]

[58] "My heart is weighed down, my soul much tormented. No, by Heaven, the Spanish foot does not beat to music on English ground."

CYPRUS
Sweet Insultado, let us see you dance.
I have heard the Spanish dance is full of state.

INSULTAD
Verdad, señor: la danza española es muy alta,
Majestica, y para monarcas: vuestra Inglesa,
Baja, fantastica, y muy humilde.[59]

[59] "The truth, sir; the Spanish dance is full of state, majestic, and fit for monarchs: your English low, fantastic, and very humble."

AGRIPYNE
Doth my Spanish prisoner deny to dance? He has sworn to me by the cross of his pure Toledo, to be my servant: by that oath, my Castilian prisoner, I conjure you to show your cunning; though all your body be not free, I am sure your heels are at liberty.

INSULTAD
Nolo quiero contra deseo; vuestro ojo hace conquista á su prisionero: Oyerer la a pavan española; sea vuestra musica y gravidad, y majestad: Paje, daime tabacco, toma my capa, y my espada. Mas alta, mas alta: Desviaios, desviaios, compañeros, mas alta, mas alta.[60] [He dances.

[60] "I desire only to please you: your eye has conquered its prisoner. You shall hear the Spanish Pavan, let your music be grave and majestic: Page, give me tobacco; take my cloak and my sword. Higher, higher: Make way, make way friends, higher, higher." The Pavan was a stately Spanish dance.

ATHELSTANE
Thanks, Insultado.

CYPRUS
'Tis most excellent.

AGRIPYNE
The Spaniard's dance is as his deeds be, full of pride.

ATHELSTANE
The day grows old, and what remains unspent,
Shall be consumed in banquets. Agripyne,
Leave us a while, if Andelocia please,
Go bear our beauteous daughter company.

ANDELOCIA
Fortune, I thank thee: now thou smil'st on me.

[Exeunt AGRIPYNE, ANDELOCIA, and LADIES.

ATHELSTANE
This Cypriot bears a gallant princely mind.
My lord, of what birth is your countryman?
Think not, sweet prince, that I propound this question,
To wrong you in your love to Agripyne:
Our favours grace him to another end.
Nor let the wings of your affection droop,
Because she seems to shun love's gentle lure.
Believe it on our word, her beauty's prize
Only shall yield a conquest to your eyes.
But tell me what's this Fortunatus' son?

CYPRUS
Of honourable blood, and more renowned
In foreign kingdoms, whither his proud spirit,
Plumed with ambitious feathers, carries him,
Than in his native country; but last day
The father and the sons were, through their riots,
Poor and disdained of all, but now they glister
More bright than Midas: if some damnèd fiend
Fed not his bags, this golden pride would end.

ATHELSTANE
His pride we'll somewhat tame, and curb the head
Of his rebellious prodigality:
He hath invited us, and all our peers,
To feast with him to-morrow; his provision,
I understand, may entertain three kings.
But Lincoln, let our subjects secretly
Be charged on pain of life that not a man
Sell any kind of fuel to his servants.

CYPRUS
This policy shall clip his golden wings,
And teach his pride what 'tis to strive with kings.

ATHELSTANE

Withdraw awhile:

[Exeunt all except ATHELSTANE.

None filled his hands with gold, for we set spies,
To watch who fed his prodigality:
He hung the marble bosom of our court,
As thick with glist'ring spangles of pure gold,
As e'er the spring hath stuck the earth with flowers.
Unless he melt himself to liquid gold,
Or be some god, some devil, or can transport
A mint about him, by enchanted power,
He cannot rain such showers. With his own hands
He threw more wealth about in every street,
Than could be thrust into a chariot.
He's a magician sure, and to some fiend,
His soul by infernal covenants has he sold,
Always to swim up to the chin in gold.
Be what he can be, if those doting fires,
Wherein he burns for Agripyne's love,
Want power to melt from him this endless mine,
Then like a slave we'll chain him in our tower,
Where tortures shall compel his sweating hands
To cast rich heaps into our treasury.

[Exit.

SCENE II.—The Same.

Music sounding still; a curtain being drawn, ANDELOCIA is discovered sleeping in AGRIPYNE'S lap; she has his purse, and she and another lady tie another like it in its place, and then rise from him.

Enter ATHELSTANE.

AGRIPYNE
I have found the sacred spring that never ebbs.
Leave us: [Exit LADY.] But I'll not show't your majesty
Till you have sworn by England's royal crown,
To let me keep it.

ATHELSTANE
By my crown I swear,
None but fair Agripyne the gem shall wear.

AGRIPYNE
Then is this mine: see, father, here's the fire

Whose gilded beams still burn, this is the sun
That ever shines, the tree that never dies,
Here grows the Garden of Hesperides;
The outside mocks you, makes you think 'tis poor,
But entering it, you find eternal store.

ATHELSTANE
Art sure of this? How didst thou drive it out?

AGRIPYNE
Fear not his waking yet, I made him drink
That soporiferous juice which was composed
To make the queen,[61] my mother, relish sleep,
When her last sickness summoned her to Heaven.
He sleeps profoundly: when his amorous eyes
Had singed their wings in Cupid's wanton flames,
I set him all on fire, and promised love,
In pride whereof, he drew me forth this purse,
And swore, by this he multiplied his gold.
I tried and found it true: and secretly
Commanded music with her silver tongue,
To chime soft lullabies into his soul,
And whilst my fingers wantoned with his hair,
T'entice the sleepy juice to charm his eyes,
In all points was there made a purse, like his,
Which counterfeit is hung in place of this.

[61] History does not record that Athelstane had either wife or daughter.

ATHELSTANE
More than a second kingdom hast thou won.
Leave him, that when he wakes he may suspect,
Some else has robbed him; come, dear Agripyne,
If this strange purse his sacred virtues hold,
We'll circle England with a wall of gold.

[Exeunt.

Music still: Enter SHADOW very gallant, reading a bill, with empty bags in his hand, singing.

SHADOW
These English occupiers are mad Trojans: let a man pay them never so much, they'll give him nothing but the bag. Since my master created me steward over his fifty men, and his one-and-fifty horse, I have rid over much business, yet never was galled, I thank the destinies. Music? O delicate warble: O these courtiers are most sweet triumphant creatures! Seignior, sir, monsieur, sweet seignior: this is the language of the accomplishment. O delicious strings; these heavenly wire-drawers have stretched my master even out at length: yet at length he must wake. Master?

ANDELOCIA
Wake me not yet, my gentle Agripyne.

SHADOW
One word, sir, for the billets, and I vanish.

ANDELOCIA
There's Heaven in these times: throw the musicians
A bounteous largesse of three hundred angels.

[ANDELOCIA starts up.

SHADOW
Why, sir, I have but ten pounds left.

ANDELOCIA
Ha, Shadow? where's the Princess Agripyne?

SHADOW
I am not Apollo, I cannot reveal.

ANDELOCIA
Was not the princess here, when thou cam'st in?

SHADOW
Here was no princess but my princely self.

ANDELOCIA
In faith?

SHADOW
No, in faith, sir.

ANDELOCIA
Where are you hid? where stand you wantoning? Not here? gone, i'faith? have you given me the slip?
Well, 'tis but an amorous trick, and so I embrace it: my horse, Shadow, how fares my horse?

SHADOW
Upon the best oats my under-steward can buy.

ANDELOCIA
I mean, are they lusty, sprightly, gallant, wanton,
fiery?

SHADOW
They are as all horses are, caterpillars to the commonwealth, they are ever munching: but, sir, for these
billets, and these fagots and bavins?

ANDELOCIA
'Sheart, what billets, what fagots? dost make me a woodmonger?

SHADOW
No, sweet seignior, but you have bid the king and his peers to dinner, and he has commanded that no woodmonger sell you a stick of wood, and that no collier shall cozn you of your measure, but must tie up the mouth of their sacks, lest their coals kindle your choler.

ANDELOCIA
Is't possible? is't true, or hast thou learnt of the
English gallants to gull?

SHADOW
He's a gull that would be taught by such gulls.

ANDELOCIA
Not a stick of wood? Some child of envy has buzzed this stratagem into the king's ear, of purpose to disgrace me. I have invited his majesty, and though it cost me a million, I'll feast him. Shadow, thou shalt hire a hundred or two of carts, with them post to all the grocers in London, buy up all the cinnamon, cloves, nutmegs, liquorice and all other spices, that have any strong heart, and with them make fires to prepare our cookery. Ere Fortunatus' son look red with shame, He'll dress a king's feast in a spicèd flame.

SHADOW
This device, sir, will be somewhat akin to Lady Pride, 'twill ask cost.

ANDELOCIA
Fetch twenty porters, I'll lade all with gold.

SHADOW
First, master, fill these bags.

ANDELOCIA
Come then, hold up. How now? tricks, new crotchets, Madame Fortune? Dry as an eel-skin? Shadow, take thou my gold out.

SHADOW
Why, sir, here's none in.

ANDELOCIA
Ha, let me see: O here's a bastard cheek,
I see now 'tis not mine; 'tis counterfeit,
'Tis so! Slave, thou hast robbed thy master.

SHADOW
Not of a penny, I have been as true a steward—

ANDELOCIA

Vengeance on thee and on thy stewardship!
Yet wherefore curse I thee? thy leaden soul
Had never power to mount up to the knowledge
Of the rich mystery closed in my purse.
Oh no, I'll curse myself, mine eyes I'll curse,
They have betrayed me; I will curse my tongue,
That hath betrayed me; I'll curse Agripyne,
She hath betrayed me. Sirens, cease to sing,
Your charms have ta'en effect, for now I see,

All your enchantments were, to cozen me.

[Music ceases.

SHADOW
What shall I do with this ten pound, sir?

ANDELOCIA
Go buy with it a chain and hang thyself.
Now think I on my father's prophecy.
Tell none, quoth he, the virtue, if you do,
Much shame, much grief, much danger follows you.
With tears I credit his divinity.
O fingers, were you upright justices,
You would tear out mine eyes! had not they gazed
On the frail colour of a painted cheek,
None had betrayed me: henceforth I'll defy
All beauty, and will call a lovely eye,
A sun whose scorching beams burn up our joys,
Or turn them black like Ethiopians.
O women, wherefore are you born men's woe,
Why are your faces framed angelical?
Your hearts of sponges, soft and smooth in show,
But touched, with poison they do overflow.
Had sacred wisdom been my father's fate,
He had died happy, I lived fortunate.
Shadow, bear this to beauteous Agripyne,
With it this message, tell her, I'll reprove
Her covetous sin the less, because for gold,
I see that most men's souls too cheap are sold.

SHADOW
Shall I buy these spices to-day or to-morrow?

ANDELOCIA
To-morrow? ay, to-morrow thou shalt buy them.
To-morrow tell the princess I will love her,
To-morrow tell the king I'll banquet him,

To-morrow, Shadow, will I give thee gold;
To-morrow pride goes bare and lust acold.
To-morrow will the rich man feed the poor,
And vice to-morrow virtue will adore.
To-morrow beggars shall be crownèd kings,
This no-time, morrow's-time, no sweetness sings:
I pray thee hence; bear that to Agripyne.

SHADOW
I'll go hence, because you send me; but I'll go weeping hence, for grief that I must turn villain as many do, and leave you when you are up to the ears in adversity.

[Exit.

ANDELOCIA
She hath robbed me, and now I'll play the thief,
Ay, steal from hence to Cyprus, for black shame
Here, through my riots, brands my lofty name.
I'll sell this pride for help to bear me thither,
So pride and beggary shall walk together.
This world is but a school of villany,
Therefore I'll rob my brother, not of gold,
Nor of his virtues, virtue none will steal—
But, if I can, I'll steal his wishing hat,
And with that, wandering round about the world,
I'll search all corners to find Misery,
And where she dwells, I'll dwell, languish and die.

[Exit.

ACT THE FOURTH.

CHORUS
Gentles, if e'er you have beheld the passions,
The combats of his soul, who being a king,
By some usurping hand hath been deposed
From all his royalties: even such a soul,
Such eyes, such heart swol'n big with sighs and tears,
The star-crossed son of Fortunatus wears.
His thoughts crowned him a monarch in the morn,
Yet now he's bandied by the seas in scorn
From wave to wave: his golden treasure's spoil
Makes him in desperate language to entreat
The winds to spend their fury on his life:
But they, being mild in tyranny, or scorning
To triumph in a wretch's funeral,

Toss him to Cyprus. Oh, what treachery
Cannot this serpent gold entice us to?
He robs his brother of the Soldan's prize,
And having got his wish, the wishing hat,
He does not, as he vowed, seek misery,
But hopes by that to win his purse again,
And in that hope from Cyprus is he fled.
If your swift thoughts clap on their wonted wings,
In Genoa may you take this fugitive,
Where having cozened many jewellers,
To England back he comes; step but to court,
And there disguised you find him bargaining
For jewels with the beauteous Agripyne,
Who wearing at her side the virtuous purse,
He clasps her in his arms, and as a raven,
Griping the tender-hearted nightingale,
So flies he with her, wishing in the air
To be transported to some wilderness:
Imagine this the place; see, here they come!
Since they themselves have tongues, mine shall be dumb.

[Exit.

SCENE I.—A Wilderness.

Enter ANDELOCIA with the wishing hat on, and dragging AGRIPYNE by the hand.

AGRIPYNE
What devil art thou that affright'st me thus,
Haling a princess from her father's court,
To spoil her in this savage wilderness?

ANDELOCIA
Indeed the devil and the pick-purse should always fly together, for they are sworn brothers: but Madam Covetousness, I am neither a devil as you call me, nor a jeweller as I call myself; no, nor a juggler,—yet ere you and I part, we'll have some legerdemain together. Do you know me?

AGRIPYNE
I am betrayed: this is the Cypriot.
Forgive me, 'twas not I that changed thy purse,
But Athelstane my father; send me home,
And here's thy purse again: here are thy jewels,
And I in satisfaction of all wrongs—

ANDELOCIA

Talk not you of satisfaction, this is some recompense, that I have you. 'Tis not the purse I regard: put it off, and I'll mince it as small as pie meat. The purse? hang the purse: were that gone, I can make another, and another, and another, ay, and another: 'tis not the purse I care for, but the purser, you, ay you. Is't not a shame that a king's daughter, a fair lady, a lady not for lords, but for monarchs, should for gold sell her love, and when she has her own asking, and that there stands nothing between, then to cheat your sweetheart? O fie, fie, a she cony-catcher? You must be dealt fondly with.

AGRIPYNE
Enjoin what pains thou wilt, and I'll endure them,
So thou wilt send me to my father's court.

ANDELOCIA
Nay God's lid, y'are not gone so: set your heart at rest, for I have set up my rest, that except you can run swifter than a hart, home you go not. What pains shall I lay upon you? Let me see: I could serve you now but a slippery touch: I could get a young king or two, or three, of you, and then send you home, and bid their grandsire king nurse them: I could pepper
you, but I will not.

AGRIPYNE
O, do not violate my chastity.

ANDELOCIA
No, why I tell you I am not given to the flesh, though I savour in your nose a little of the devil, I could run away else, and starve you here.

AGRIPYNE
If I must die, doom me some easier death.

ANDELOCIA
Or transform you, because you love picking, into a squirrel, and make you pick out a poor living here among the nut trees: but I will not neither.

AGRIPYNE
What will my gentle Andelocia do?

ANDELOCIA
Oh, now you come to your old bias of cogging.[394]

[394] Your old mind (or, more literally, inclination) of cajoling.

AGRIPYNE
I pray thee, Andelocia, let me go:
Send me to England, and by Heaven I swear,
Thou from all kings on earth my love shalt bear.

ANDELOCIA
Shall I in faith?

AGRIPYNE
In faith, in faith thou shalt.

ANDELOCIA
Hear, God a mercy: now thou shalt not go.

AGRIPYNE
Oh God.

ANDELOCIA
Nay, do you hear, lady? Cry not, y'are best; no nor curse me not. If you think but a crabbed thought of me, the spirit that carried you in mine arms through the air, will tell me all; therefore set your Sunday face upon't. Since you'll love me, I'll love you, I'll marry you, and lie with you, and beget little jugglers: marry, home you get not. England, you'll say, is yours: but, Agripyne, love me, and I will make the whole world thine.

AGRIPYNE
I care not for the world, thou murd'rest me;
Between my sorrow, and the scalding sun
I faint, and quickly will my life be done,
My mouth is like a furnace, and dry heat
Drinks up my blood. O God, my heart will burst,
I die, unless some moisture quench my thirst.

ANDELOCIA
'Sheart, now I am worse than ere I was before:
For half the world I would not have her die.
Here's neither spring nor ditch, nor rain, nor dew,
Nor bread nor drink: my lovely Agripyne,
Be comforted, see here are apple trees.

AGRIPYNE
Climb up for God's sake, reach me some of them.

ANDELOCIA
Look up, which of these apples likes thee best?

AGRIPYNE
This hath a withered face, 'tis some sweet fruit.
Not that, my sorrows are too sour already.

ANDELOCIA
Come hither, here are apples like gold.

AGRIPYNE
O, ay, for God's sake, gather some of these.
Ay me, would God I were at home again!

ANDELOCIA
Stand farther, lest I chance to fall on thee.

[Climbs up.

Oh here be rare apples, rare red-cheeked apples, that cry come kiss me: apples, hold your peace, I'll teach you to cry.

[Eats one.

AGRIPYNE
O England, shall I ne'er behold thee more?

ANDELOCIA
Agripyne, 'tis a most sugared delicious taste in one's mouth, but when 'tis down, 'tis as bitter as gall.

AGRIPYNE
Yet gather some of them. Oh, that a princess
Should pine for food: were I at home again,
I should disdain to stand thus and complain.

ANDELOCIA
Here's one apple that grows highest, Agripyne; an' I could reach that, I'll come down.

[Fishes with his girdle for it.

AGRIPYNE
Make haste, for the hot sun doth scald my cheeks.

ANDELOCIA
The sun kiss thee? hold, catch, put on my hat, I will have yonder highest apple, though I die for't.

AGRIPYNE
I had not wont be sun-burnt, wretched me.
O England, would I were again in thee!

[Exit.

ANDELOCIA leaps down.

ANDELOCIA
'Swounds, Agripyne, stay, Oh I am undone!
Sweet Agripyne, if thou hear'st my voice,
Take pity of me, and return again.
She flies like lightning: Oh she hears me not!
I wish myself into a wilderness,
And now I shall turn wild: here I shall famish,
Here die, here cursing die, here raving die,

And thus will wound my breast, and rend mine hair.
What hills of flint are grown upon my brows?
O me, two forkèd horns, I am turned beast,
I have abused two blessings, wealth and knowledge,
Wealth in my purse, and knowledge in my hat,
By which being borne into the courts of kings,
I might have seen the wondrous works of Jove,
Acquired experience, learning, wisdom, truth,
But I in wildness tottered out my youth,
And therefore must turn wild, must be a beast,
An ugly beast: my body horns must bear,
Because my soul deformity doth wear.
Lives none within this wood? If none but I
Live here,—thanks Heaven! for here none else shall die.

[Lies down and sleeps under the tree.

Enter FORTUNE, VICE, VIRTUE, the PRIEST: and SATYRS with music, playing before FORTUNE

FORTUNE
See where my new-turned devil has built his hell.

VICE
Virtue, who conquers now? the fool is ta'en.

VIRTUE
O sleepy sin.

VICE
Sweet tunes, wake him again.

[Music sounds awhile, and then ceases.

FORTUNE
Vice sits too heavy on his drowsy soul,
Music's sweet concord cannot pierce his ear.
Sing, and amongst your songs mix bitter scorn.

VIRTUE
Those that tear Virtue, must by Vice be torn.

SONG.

Virtue, stand aside: the fool is caught.
Laugh to see him, laugh aloud to wake him;
Folly's nets are wide, and neatly wrought,
Mock his horns, and laugh to see Vice take him.

CHORUS
Ha, ha, ha, ha, ha, laugh, laugh in scorn,
Who's the fool? the fool, he wears a horn.

[ANDELOCIA wakens and stands up.

Virtue, stand aside, mock him, mock him, mock him,
Laugh aloud to see him, call him fool.
Error gave him suck, now sorrows rock him,
Send the riotous beast to madness' school.

CHORUS
Ha, ha, ha, ha, ha, laugh, laugh in scorn.
Who's the fool? the fool, he wears a horn.

Virtue, stand aside: your school he hates.
Laugh aloud to see him, mock, mock, mock him.
Vanity and hell keep open gates,
He's in, and a new nurse, Despair, must rock him.

CHORUS
Ha, ha, ha, ha, ha, laugh, laugh in scorn,
Fool, fool, fool, fool, fool, wear still the horn.

[VICE and VIRTUE hold apples out to ANDELOCIA, VICE laughing, VIRTUE grieving.

ANDELOCIA
O me, what hell is this? fiends, tempt me not.
Thou glorious devil, hence. O now I see,
This fruit is thine, thou hast deformèd me:
Idiot, avoid, thy gifts I loathe to taste.
Away: since I am entered madness' school,
As good to be a beast, as be a fool.
Away, why tempt you me? some powerful grace
Come and redeem me from this hideous place.

FORTUNE
To her hath Andelocia all his life
Sworn fealty; would'st thou forsake her now?

ANDELOCIA
Whose blessed tongue names Andelocia?

FORTUNE
Hers, who, attended on by destinies,
Shortened thy father's life, and lengthens thine.

ANDELOCIA

O sacred Queen of chance, now shorten mine,
Else let thy deity take off this shame.

FORTUNE
Woo her, 'twas she that set it on thy head.

ANDELOCIA
She laughs to see me metamorphosèd.

[Rises.

VIRTUE
Woo me, and I'll take off this ugly scorn.

VICE
Woo me, and I'll clap on another horn.

ANDELOCIA
I am beset with anguish, shame and death.
O bid the Fates work fast, and stop my breath.

FORTUNE
No, Andelocia, thou must live to see
Worse torments, for thy follies, light on thee.
This golden tree, which did thine eyes entice,
Was planted here by Vice: lo, here stands Vice:
How often hast thou sued to win her grace?

ANDELOCIA
Till now, I never did behold her face.

FORTUNE
Thou didst behold her at thy father's death,
When thou in scorn didst violate his will;
Thou didst behold her, when thy stretched-out arm
Catched at the highest bough, the loftiest vice,
The fairest apple, but the foulest price;
Thou didst behold her, when thy liquorish eye
Fed on the beauty of fair Agripyne;
Because th' hadst gold, thou thought'st all women thine.
When look'st thou off from her? for they whose souls
Still revel in the nights of vanity,
On the fair cheeks of Vice still fix their eye.
Because her face doth shine, and all her bosom
Bears silver moons, thou wast enamoured of her.
But hadst thou upward looked, and seen these shames,
Or viewed her round about, and in this glass
Seen idiots' faces, heads of devils and hell,

And read this "Ha, ha, he," this merry story,
Thou wouldst have loathed her: where, by loving her,
Thou bear'st this face, and wear'st this ugly head,
And if she once can bring thee to this place,
Loud sounds these "Ha, ha, he!" She'll laugh apace.

ANDELOCIA
O, re-transform me to a glorious shape,
And I will learn how I may love to hate her.

FORTUNE
I cannot re-transform thee, woo this woman.

ANDELOCIA
This woman? wretched is my state, when I,
To find out wisdom, to a fool must fly.

FORTUNE
Fool, clear thine eyes, this is bright Aretë,[62]
This is poor virtue, care not how the world
Doth crown her head, the world laughs her to scorn,
Yet "SIBI SAPIT," Virtue knows her worth.
Run after her, she'll give thee these and these,
Crowns and bay-garlands, honour's victories:
Serve her, and she will fetch thee pay from Heaven,
Or give thee some bright office in the stars.

[62] Virtue. Greek.

ANDELOCIA
Immortal Aretë, Virtue divine:

[Kneels.

O smile on me, and I will still be thine.

VIRTUE
Smile thou on me, and I will still be thine:
Though I am jealous of thy apostasy,
I'll entertain thee: here, come taste this tree,
Here's physic for thy sick deformity.

ANDELOCIA
Tis bitter: this fruit I shall ne'er digest.

VIRTUE
Try once again, the bitterness soon dies.

VICE
Mine's sweet, taste mine.

VIRTUE
But being down 'tis sour,
And mine being down has a delicious taste.
The path that leads to Virtue's court is narrow,
Thorny and up a hill, a bitter journey,
But being gone through, you find all heavenly sweets,
The entrance is all flinty, but at th' end,
To towers of pearl and crystal you ascend.

ANDELOCIA
O delicate, O sweet Ambrosian relish,
And see, my ugliness drops from my brows,
Thanks, beauteous Aretë: O had I now
My hat and purse again, how I would shine,
And gild my soul with none but thoughts divine.

FORTUNE
That shall be tried, take fruit from both these trees,
By help of them, win both thy purse and hat,
I will instruct thee how, for on my wings
To England shalt thou ride; thy virtuous brother
Is, with that Shadow who attends on thee,
In London, there I'll set thee presently.
But if thou lose our favours once again,
To taste her sweets, those sweets must prove
thy bane.

VIRTUE
Vice, who shall now be crowned with victory?

VICE
She that triumphs at last, and that must I.

[Exeunt.

SCENE II.—London. The Court of Athelstane

Enter ATHELSTANE, LINCOLN with AGRIPYNE, CYPRUS, GALLOWAY, CORNWALL, CHESTER, LONGAVILLE and MONTROSE.

ATHELSTANE
Lincoln, how set'st thou her at liberty?

LINCOLN
No other prison held her but your court,
There in her chamber hath she hid herself
These two days, only to shake off that fear,
Which her late violent rapture cast upon her.

CYPRUS
Where hath the beauteous Agripyne been?

AGRIPYNE
In Heaven or hell, in or without the world,
I know not which, for as I oft have seen,
When angry Thamesis hath curled her locks,
A whirlwind come, and from her frizzled brows,
Snatch up a handful of those sweaty pearls,
That stood upon her forehead, which awhile,
Being by the boist'rous wind hung in the air,
At length hath flung them down and raised a storm,—
Even with such fury was I wherried up,
And by such force held prisoner in the clouds,
And thrown by such a tempest down again.

CORNWALL
Some soul is damned in hell for this black deed.

AGRIPYNE
I have the purse safe, and anon your grace
Shall hear the wondrous history at full.

CYPRUS
Tell me, tormentor, shall fair Agripyne,
Without more difference be now christened mine!

AGRIPYNE
My choice must be my father's fair consent.

ATHELSTANE
Then shall thy choice end in this Cyprus prince.
Before the sun shall six times more arise,
His royal marriage will we solemnise.
Proclaim this honoured match! Come, Agripyne,
I am glad th' art here, more glad the purse is mine.

[As they are going in, enter ANDELOCIA and SHADOW, disguised as Irish coster-mongers. AGRIPYNE, LONGAVILLE, and MONTROSE stay listening to them, the rest exeunt.

BOTH
Buy any apples, feene apples of Tamasco,[63] feene

Tamasco peepins: peeps feene, buy Tamasco peepins.

[63] In the English translation from the original story of Fortunatus, as published in the Dutch, Andelocia invents the name of Damascus, or Damasco, for his apples, on the spur of the moment, so as to give them an air of rarety, the name apparently not being one previously used for any special kind of apple. In an earlier English edition of the story, published about 1650, however, they are otherwise described. It says there:—"They were brought from Jerusalem, and were from the Holy Garden."

AGRIPYNE
Damasco apples? good my Lord Montrose,
Call yonder fellows.

MONTROSE
Sirrah coster-monger.

SHADOW
Who calls: peeps of Tamasco, feene peeps: Ay, fat 'tis de sweetest apple in de world, 'tis better den de Pome water,[64] or apple John.[65]

[64] A large sweet apple, full of juice [see Bailey's Dictionary].

[65] John apple, a good keeping apple, which long retains its freshness.

ANDELOCIA
By my trat, madam, 'tis reet Tamasco peepins, look here els.

SHADOW
I dare not say, as de Irishman my countryman say, taste de goodness of de fruit: no, sayt, 'tis farie teere, mistriss, by Saint Patrick's hand 'tis teere Tamasco apple.

AGRIPYNE
The fairest fruit that ever I beheld.
Damasco apples, wherefore are they good?

LONGAVILLE
What is your price of half a score of these?

Both. Half a score, half a score? dat is doos many,
mester.[66]

[66] "That is too many, master." Dekker's Irish even surpasses his Dutch in unintelligibility, and it would need more space than mere footnotes can afford, to attempt any full elucidation.

LONGAVILLE
Ay, ay, ten, half a score, that's five and five.

ANDELOCIA

Feeve and feeve? By my trat and as Creeze save me la, I cannot tell wat be de price of feeve and feeve, but 'tis tree crown for one peepin, dat is de preez if you take 'em.

SHADOW
Ay fat, 'tis no less for Tamasco.

AGRIPYNE
Three crowns for one? what wondrous virtues have they?

SHADOW
O, 'tis feene Tamasco apple, and shall make you a great teal wise, and make you no fool, and make feene memory.

ANDELOCIA
And make dis fash be more fair and amiable, and make dis eyes look always lovely, and make all de court and country burn in desire to kiss di none sweet countenance.

MONTROSE
Apples to make a lady beautiful?
Madam, that's excellent.

AGRIPYNE
These Irishmen,
Some say, are great dissemblers, and I fear
These two the badge of their own country wear.

ANDELOCIA
By my trat, and by Saint Patrick's hand, and as Creez save me la, 'tis no dissembler: de Irishman now and den cut di countryman's throat, but yet in fayt he love di countryman, 'tis no dissembler: dis feene Tamasco apple can make di sweet countenance, but I can take no less but three crowns for one, I wear out my naked legs and my foots, and my tods,[67] and run hidder and didder to Tamasco for dem.

[67] Stockings probably, from the use of the term for bales of wool.

SHADOW
As Creez save me la, he speaks true: Peeps feene.

AGRIPYNE
I'll try what power lies in Damasco fruit.
Here are ten crowns for three. So fare you well.

MONTROSE
Lord Longaville, buy some.

LONGAVILLE
I buy? not I:
Hang them, they are toys; come, madam, let us go.

[Exeunt AGRIPYNE, LONGAVILLE and MONTROSE.

BOTH
Saint Patrick and Saint Peter, and all de holy angels look upon dat fash and make it fair.

Re-enter MONTROSE softly.

SHADOW
Ha, ha, ha! she's sped, I warrant.

ANDELOCIA
Peace, Shadow, buy any peepins, buy.

Both. Peeps feene, feene Tamasco apples.

MONTROSE
Came not Lord Longaville to buy some fruit?

ANDELOCIA
No fat, master, here came no lords nor ladies, but di none sweet self.

MONTROSE
'Tis well, say nothing, here's six crowns for two:
You say the virtues are to make one strong.

BOTH
Yes fat, and make sweet countenance and strong too.

MONTROSE
'Tis excellent: here! farewell! if these prove,
I'll conquer men by strength, women by love.

[Exit.

Re-enter LONGAVILLE.

ANDELOCIA
Ha, ha, ha! why this is rare.

SHADOW
Peace, master, here comes another fool.

BOTH
Peepes feene, buy any peepes of Tamasco?

LONGAVILLE
Did not the Lord Montrose return to you?

BOTH
No fat, sweet master, no lord did turn to us: peepes feene!

LONGAVILLE
I am glad of it; here are nine crowns for three.
What are the virtues besides making fair?

ANDELOCIA
O, 'twill make thee wondrous wise.

SHADOW
And dow shall be no more a fool, but sweet face and wise.

LONGAVILLE
'Tis rare, farewell, I never yet durst woo.
None loves me: now I'll try what these can do.

[Exit.

ANDELOCIA
Ha, ha, ha. So, this is admirable, Shadow, here end my torments in Saint Patrick's Purgatory, but thine shall continue longer.

SHADOW
Did I not clap on a good false Irish face?

ANDELOCIA
It became thee rarely.

SHADOW
Yet that's lamentable, that a false face should become any man.

ANDELOCIA
Thou art a gull,[68] tis all the fashion now, which fashion because we'll keep, step thou abroad, let not the world want fools; whilst thou art commencing thy knavery there, I'll precede Dr. Dodipoll[69] here: that done, thou, Shadow, and I will fat ourselves[70] to behold the transformation of these fools: go fly.

[68] Dekker uses "Gallant," as an equivalent in The Gull's Horn-Book, but he means something more opprobrious;—"Masher," as we would say to-day, a fool of fashion.

[69] An allusion to the comedy The Wisdom of Dr. Dodipoll.

[70] i.e. Grow jolly, at the spectacle.

SHADOW
I fear nothing, but that whilst we strive to make others fools, we shall wear the cock's combs ourselves. Pips fine.

[Exit SHADOW.

Enter AMPEDO.

ANDELOCIA
S'heart, here's my brother whom I have abused:
His presence makes me blush, it strikes me dead,
To think how I am metamorphosèd.
Feene peepins of Tamasco!

AMPEDO
For shame cast off this mask.

ANDELOCIA
Wilt thou buy any pips?

AMPEDO
Mock me no longer
With idle apparitions: many a land
Have I with weary feet and a sick soul
Measured to find thee; and when thou art found,
My greatest grief is that thou art not lost.
Yet lost thou art, thy fame, thy wealth are lost,
Thy wits are lost, and thou hast in their stead,
With shame and cares, and misery crowned thy head.
That Shadow that pursues thee, filled mine ears
With sad relation of thy wretchedness,
Where is the purse, and where my wishing hat?

ANDELOCIA
Where, and where? are you created constable? You stand so much upon interrogatories. The purse is gone, let that fret you, and the hat is gone, let that mad you: I run thus through all trades to overtake them, if you be quiet, follow me, and help, if not, fly from me, and hang yourself. Wilt thou buy any pippins?

[Exit.

AMPEDO
Oh, how I grieve, to see him thus transformed?
Yet from the circles of my jealous eyes
He shall not start, till he have repossessed
Those virtuous jewels, which found once again,
More cause they ne'er shall give me to complain,
Their worth shall be consumed in murdering flames,
And end my grief, his riot, and our shames.

[Exit.

ACT THE FIFTH.

SCENE I.—London. The Court of Athelstane.

Enter ATHELSTANE, followed by AGRIPYNE, MONTROSE, and LONGAVILLE with horns; then LINCOLN and CORNWALL.

ATHELSTANE
In spite of sorcery try once again,
Try once more in contempt of all damned spells.

AGRIPYNE
Your majesty fights with no mortal power.
Shame, and not conquest, hangs upon this strife.
O, touch me not, you add but pain to pain,
The more you cut, the more they grow again.

LINCOLN
Is there no art to conjure down this scorn?
I ne'er knew physic yet against the horn.

Enter CYPRUS.

ATHELSTANE
See, Prince of Cyprus, thy fair Agripyne
Hath turned her beauty to deformity.

CYPRUS
Then I defy thee, Love; vain hopes, adieu,
You have mocked me long; in scorn I'll now mock you.
I came to see how the Lord Longaville
Was turned into a monster, and I find
An object, which both strikes me dumb and blind.
To-morrow should have been our marriage morn,
But now my bride is shame, thy bridegroom scorn.
tell me yet, is there no art, no charms,
No desperate physic for this desperate wound?

ATHELSTANE
All means are tried, but no means can be found.

CYPRUS
Then, England, farewell: hapless maid, thy stars,
Through spiteful influence set our hearts at wars.
I am enforced to leave thee, and resign
My love to grief.

Enter ORLEANS and GALLOWAY.

AGRIPYNE
All grief to Agripyne.

CYPRUS
Adieu, I would say more, had I a tongue
Able to help his master: mighty king,
I humbly take my leave; to Cyprus I;
My father's son must all such shame defy.

[Exit.

ORLEANS
So doth not Orleans; I defy all those
That love not Agripyne, and him defy,
That dares but love her half so well as I.
O pardon me! I have in sorrow's jail
Been long tormented, long this mangled bosom
Hath bled, and never durst expose her wounds,
Till now, till now, when at thy beauteous feet
I offer love and life. Oh, cast an eye
Of mercy on me, this deformèd face
Cannot affright my soul from loving thee.

AGRIPYNE
Talk not of love, good Orleans, but of hate.

ORLEANS
What sentence will my love pronounce on me?

GALLOWAY
Will Orleans then be mad? O gentle friend.

ORLEANS
O gentle, gentle friend, I am not mad:
He's mad, whose eyes on painted cheeks do doat,
O Galloway, such read beauty's book by rote.
He's mad, that pines for want of a gay flower,
Which fades when grief doth blast, or sickness lower,
Which heat doth wither, and white age's frost
Nips dead: such fairness, when 'tis found, 'tis lost.
I am not mad, for loving Agripyne,
My love looks on her eyes with eyes divine;
I doat on the rich brightness of her mind,
That sacred beauty strikes all other blind.
O make me happy then, since my desires

Are set a burning by love's purest fires.

ATHELSTANE
So thou wilt bear her far from England's sight,
Enjoy thy wishes.

AGRIPYNE
Lock me in some cave,
Where staring wonder's eye shall not be guilty
To my abhorrèd looks, and I will die
To thee, as full of love as misery.

ATHELSTANE
I am amazed and mad, some speckled soul
Lies pawned for this in hell, without redemption,
Some fiend deludes us all.

CORNWALL
O unjust Fates,
Why do you hide from us this mystery?

LINCOLN
My Lord Montrose, how long have your brows worn
This fashion? these two feather springs of horn?

MONTROSE
An Irish kerne sold me Damasco apples
Some two hours since, and like a credulous fool—
He swearing to me that they had this power
To make me strong in body, rich in mind—
I did believe his words, tasted his fruit,
And since have been attired in this disguise.

LONGAVILLE
I fear that villain hath beguiled me too.

CORNWALL
Nay before God he has not cozened you,
You have it soundly.

LONGAVILLE
Me he made believe,
One apple of Damasco would inspire
My thoughts with wisdom, and upon my cheeks
Would cast such beauty that each lady's eye,
Which looked on me, should love me presently.

AGRIPYNE

Desire to look more fair, makes me more fool,[71]
Those apples did entice my wandering eye,
To be enamoured of deformity.

[71] A play upon "fool" and "foul."

ATHELSTANE
This proves that true, which oft I have heard in schools,
Those that would seem most wise, do turn most fools.

LINCOLN
Here's your best hope, none needs to hide his face,
For hornèd foreheads swarm in every place.

Enter CHESTER, with ANDELOCIA disguised as a French Soldier.

ATHELSTANE
Now, Chester, what physicians hast thou found?

CHESTER
Many, my liege, but none that have true skill
To tame such wild diseases: yet here's one,
A doctor and a Frenchman, whom report
Of Agripyne's grief hath drawn to court.

ATHELSTANE
Cure her, and England's treasury shall stand,
As free for thee to use, as rain from Heaven.

MONTROSE
Cure me, and to thy coffers I will send
More gold from Scotland than thy life can spend.

LONGAVILLE
Cure Longaville, and all his wealth is thine.

ANDELOCIA
He Monsieur Long-villain,[72] gra tanck you: Gra tanck your mashesty a great teal artely by my trat: where be dis Madam Princeza dat be so mush tormenta? O Jeshu: one, two: an tree, four an five, seez horn: Ha, ha, ha, pardona moy prea wid al mine art, for by my trat, me can no point shose but laugh, Ha, ha, ha, to mark how like tree bul-beggera, dey stand. Oh, by my trat and fat, di divela be whoreson, scurvy, paltry, ill favore knave to mock de madam, and gentill-home so: Ha, ha, ha, ha.

[72] Elucidation of his jargon must be left to the discretion of the reader.

LINCOLN
This doctor comes to mock your majesty.

ANDELOCIA
No, by my trat la, but me lova musha musha merymant: come, madam, pre-artely stand still, and letta me feel you. Dis horn, O 'tis pretty horn, dis be facile, easy for pull de vey; but, madam, dis O be grand, grand horn, difficil, and very deep; 'tis perilous, a grand laroone. But, madam, prea be patient, we shall take it off vell.

ATHELSTANE
Thrice have we pared them off, but with fresh pain,
In compass of a thought they rise again.

ANDELOCIA
It's true, 'tis no easy mattra, to pull horn off, 'tis easy to pull on, but hard for pull off; some horn be so good fellow, he will still inhabit in de man's pate, but 'tis all one for tat, I shall snap away all dis. Madam, trust dis down into your little belly.

AGRIPYNE
Father, I am in fear to taste his physic.
First let him work experiments on those.

ANDELOCIA
I'll sauce you for your infidelity.
In no place can I spy my wishing hat.   [Aside.

LONGAVILLE
Thou learned Frenchman, try thy skill on me,
More ugly than I am, I cannot be.

MONTROSE
Cure me, and Montrose wealth shall all be thine.

ANDELOCIA
'Tis all one for dat! Shall do presently, madam, prea mark me. Monsieur, shamp dis in your two shaps, so, now Monsieur Long-villain; dis so; now dis; fear noting, 'tis eshelent medicine! so, now cram dis into your guts, and belly; so, now snap away dis whoreson four divela; Ha, ha, is no point good?

[Pulls LONGAVILLE'S horns off.

ATHELSTANE
This is most strange.
Was't painful, Longaville?

LONGAVILLE
Ease took them off, and there remains no pain.

AGRIPYNE
O try thy sacred physic upon me.

ANDELOCIA

No by my trat, 'tis no possibla, 'tis no possibla, al de mattra, all de ting, all de substance, all de medicine, be among his and his belly: 'tis no possibla, till me prepare more.

ATHELSTANE
Prepare it then, and thou shalt have more gold
From England's coffers, than thy life can waste.

ANDELOCIA
I must buy many costly tings, dat grow in Arabia, in Asia, and America, by my trat 'tis no possibla till anoder time, no point.

AGRIPYNE
There's nothing in the world, but may for gold
Be bought in England; hold your lap, I'll rain
A shower of angels.

ANDELOCIA
Fie, fie, fie, fie, you no credit le dockature? Ha, but vel, 'tis all one for tat: 'tis no mattera for gold! vel, vel, vel, vel, vel, me have some more, prea say noting, shall be presently prepara for your horns.

(Aside.) She has my purse, and yonder lies my hat,
Work, brains, and once more make me fortunate.—

Vel, vel, vel, vel, be patient, madam, presently, presently! Be patient, me have two, tree, four and five medicines for de horn: presently, madam, stand you der, prea wid all my art, stand you all der, and say noting,—so! nor look noting dis vey. So, presently, presently, madam, snip dis horn off wid de rushes and anoder ting by and by, by and by, by and by. Prea look none dis vey, and say noting. [Takes his hat.

ATHELSTANE
Let no man speak, or look, upon his life.
Doctor, none here shall rob thee of thy skill.

ANDELOCIA
So, taka dis hand: winck now prea artely with your two nyes: why so.

Would I were with my brother Ampedo!

[Exit with AGRIPYNE.

AGRIPYNE
Help, father, help, I am hurried hence perforce.

ATHELSTANE
Draw weapons, where's the princess? follow him,
Stay the French doctor, stay the doctor there.

[CORNWALL and others run out, and presently re-enter.

CORNWALL
Stay him! 's heart, who dare stay him? 'tis the devil
In likeness of a Frenchman, of a doctor.
Look how a rascal kite having swept up
A chicken in his claws, so flies this hell-hound
In th' air with Agripyne in his arms.

ORLEANS
Mount every man upon his swiftest horse.
Fly several ways, he cannot bear her far.

GALLOWAY
These paths we'll beat.

[Exeunt GALLOWAY and ORLEANS.

LINCOLN
And this way shall be mine.

[Exit.

CORNWALL
This way, my liege, I'll ride.

[Exit.

ATHELSTANE
And this way I:
No matter which way, to seek misery.

[Exit.

LONGAVILLE
I can ride no way, to out-run my shame.

MONTROSE
Yes, Longaville, let's gallop after too;
Doubtless this doctor was that Irish devil,
That cozened us, the medicine which he gave us
Tasted like his Damasco villany.
To horse, to horse, if we can catch this fiend,
Our forkèd shame shall in his heart blood end.

LONGAVILLE
O how this mads me, that all tongues in scorn,
Which way soe'er I ride, cry, 'ware the horn!

[Exeunt.

SCENE II.—An open Space near London: a Prison and a Pair of Stocks in the background.

Enter ANDELOCIA with AGRIPYNE, AMPEDO and SHADOW following.

AGRIPYNE
O gentle Andelocia, pity me,
Take off this infamy, or take my life.

ANDELOCIA
Your life? you think then that I am a true doctor indeed, that tie up my living in the knots of winding sheets: your life? no, keep your life, but deliver your purse: you know the thief's salutation,—"Stand and deliver." So, this is mine, and these yours: I'll teach you to live by the sweat of other men's brows.

SHADOW
And to strive to be fairer than God made her.

ANDELOCIA
Right, Shadow: therefore vanish, you have made me turn juggler, and cry "hey-pass," but your horns shall not repass.[73]

[73] "They mean to fall to their hey-pass and re-pass."

AGRIPYNE
O gentle Andelocia.

ANDELOCIA
Andelocia is a nettle: if you touch him gently, he'll sting you.

SHADOW
Or a rose: if you pull his sweet stalk he'll prick you.

ANDELOCIA
Therefore not a word; go, trudge to your father. Sigh not for your purse, money may be got by you, as well as by the little Welshwoman in Cyprus, that had but one horn in her head;[74] you have two, and perhaps you shall cast both. As you use me, mark those words well, "as you use me," nay, y'are best fly, I'll not endure one word more. Yet stay too, because you entreat me so gently, and that I'll make some amends to your father,—although I care not for any king in Christendom, yet hold you, take this apple, eat it as you go to court, and your horns shall play the cowards and fall from you.

[74] A reference probably to a woman exhibited at some show in London, and transferred by Dekker, with his usual artistic liberty, to Cyprus.

AGRIPYNE
O gentle Andelocia.

ANDELOCIA
Nay, away, not a word.

SHADOW
Ha, ha, ha! 'Ware horns!

[Exit AGRIPYNE, weeping.

ANDELOCIA
Why dost thou laugh, Shadow?

SHADOW
To see what a horn plague follows covetousness and pride.

AMPEDO
Brother, what mysteries lie in all this?

ANDELOCIA
Tricks, Ampedo, tricks, devices, and mad hieroglyphics, mirth, mirth, and melody. O, there's more music in this, than all the gamut airs, and sol fa res, in the world; here's the purse, and here's the hat: because you shall be sure I'll not start, wear you this, you know its virtue. If danger beset you, fly and away: a sort of broken-shinned limping-legged jades run hobbling to seek us. Shadow, we'll for all this have one fit of mirth more, to make us laugh and be fat.

SHADOW
And when we are fat, master, we'll do as all gluttons do, laugh and lie down.

ANDELOCIA
Hie thee to my chamber, make ready my richest attire,
I'll to court presently.

SHADOW
I'll go to court in this attire, for apparel is but the shadow of a man, but shadow is the substance of his apparel.

[Exit SHADOW.

ANDELOCIA
Away, away, and meet me presently.

AMPEDO
I had more need to cry away to thee.
Away, away with this wild lunacy,
Away with riots.

ANDELOCIA
Away with your purity, brother, y'are an ass. Why doth this purse spit out gold but to be spent? why lives a man in this world, to dwell in the suburbs of it, as you do? Away, foreign simplicity, away: are not

eyes made to see fair ladies? hearts to love them? tongues to court them, and hands to feel them? Out, you stock, you stone, you log's end: Are not legs made to dance, and shall mine limp up and down the world after your cloth-stocking-heels? You have the hat, keep it. Anon I'll visit your virtuous countenance again; adieu! Pleasure is my sweet mistress, I wear her love in my hat, and her soul in my heart: I have sworn to be merry, and in spite of Fortune and the black-browed Destinies, I'll never be sad.

[Exit.

AMPEDO
Go, fool; in spite of mirth, thou shalt be sad.
I'll bury half thy pleasures in a grave
Of hungry flames; this fire I did ordain
To burn both purse and hat: as this doth perish,
So shall the other; count what good and bad
They both have wrought, the good is to the ill
As a small pebble to a mighty hill.
Thy glory and thy mischiefs here shall burn;
Good gifts abused to man's confusion turn.

Enter LONGAVILLE and MONTROSE with Soldiers.

LONGAVILLE
This is his brother: soldiers, bind his arms.

MONTROSE
Bind arms and legs, and hale the fiend away.

AMPEDO
Uncivil: wherefore must I taste your spite?

LONGAVILLE
Art thou not one of Fortunatus' sons?

AMPEDO
I am, but he did never do you wrong.

LONGAVILLE
The devil thy brother has; villain, look here.

MONTROSE
Where is the beauteous purse and wishing hat?

AMPEDO
My brother Andelocia has the purse,
This way he'll come anon to pass to court.
Alas, that sin should make men's hearts so bold,
To kill their souls for the base thirst of gold.

The wishing hat is burnt.

MONTROSE
Burnt? Soldiers, bind him.
Tortures shall wring both hat and purse from you.
Villain, I'll be revenged for that base scorn
Thy hell-hound brother clapped upon my head.

LONGAVILLE
And so will Longaville.
Away with him!

MONTROSE
Drag him to yonder tower, there shackle him,
And in a pair of stocks lock up his heels,
And bid your wishing cap deliver you.
Give us the purse and hat, we'll set thee free,
Else rot to death and starve.

AMPEDO
Oh tyranny, you need not scorn the badge which you did bear:
Beasts would you be, though horns you did not wear.

MONTROSE
Drag hence the cur: come, noble Longaville,
One's sure, and were the other fiend as fast,
Their pride should cost their lives: their purse and hat
Shall both be ours, we'll share them equally.

LONGAVILLE
That will be some amends for arming me.

Enter ANDELOCIA, and SHADOW after him.

MONTROSE
Peace, Longaville, yonder the gallant comes.

LONGAVILLE
Y'are well encountered.

ANDELOCIA
Thanks, Lord Longaville.

LONGAVILLE
The king expects your presence at the court.

ANDELOCIA
And thither am I going.

SHADOW
Pips fine, fine apples of Tamasco, ha, ha, ha!

MONTROSE
Wert thou that Irishman that cozened us?

SHADOW
Pips fine, ha, ha, ha! no not I: not Shadow.

ANDELOCIA
Were not your apples delicate and rare?

LONGAVILLE
The worst that e'er you sold; sirs, bind him fast.

ANDELOCIA
What, will you murder me? help, help, some help!

SHADOW
Help, help, help!

[Exit SHADOW.

MONTROSE
Follow that dog, and stop his bawling throat.

ANDELOCIA
Villains, what means this barbarous treachery?

LONGAVILLE
We mean to be revenged for our disgrace.

MONTROSE
And stop the golden current of thy waste.

ANDELOCIA
Murder! they murder me, O call for help.

LONGAVILLE
Thy voice is spent in vain; come, come, this purse,
This well-spring of your prodigality.

ANDELOCIA
Are you appointed by the king to this?

MONTROSE
No, no; rise, spurn him up! know you who's this?

ANDELOCIA
My brother Ampedo? Alas, what fate
Hath made thy virtues so unfortunate?

AMPEDO
Thy riot and the wrong of these two lords,
Who causeless thus do starve[75] me in this prison.

[75] This is an imaginative prevision on the part of Ampedo, as again in his next speech, "My want is famine."

LONGAVILLE
Strive not y'are best, villains, lift in his legs.

ANDELOCIA
Traitors to honour, what do you intend?

LONGAVILLE
That riot shall in wretchedness have end.
Question thy brother with what cost he's fed,
And so assure thou shall be banqueted.

[Exeunt LONGAVILLE and MONTROSE.

AMPEDO
In want, in misery, in woe and care,
Poor Ampedo his fill hath surfeited:
My want is famine, bolts my misery,
My care and woe should be thy portion.

ANDELOCIA
Give me that portion, for I have a heart
Shall spend it freely, and make bankrupt
The proudest woe that ever wet man's eyes.
Care, with a mischief! wherefore should I care?
Have I rid side by side by mighty kings,
Yet be thus bridled now? I'll tear these fetters,
Murder! cry, murder! Ampedo, aloud.
To bear this scorn our fortunes are too proud.

AMPEDO
O folly, thou hast power to make flesh glad,
When the rich soul in wretchedness is clad.

ANDELOCIA
Peace, fool, am I not Fortune's minion?
These bands are but one wrinkle of her frown,

This is her evening mask, her next morn's eye
Shall overshine the sun in majesty.

AMPEDO
But this sad night will make an end of me.
Brother, farewell; grief, famine, sorrow, want,
Have made an end of wretched Ampedo.

ANDELOCIA
Where is the wishing hat?

AMPEDO
Consumed in fire.

ANDELOCIA
Accursèd be those hands that did destroy it;
That would redeem us, did we now enjoy it.

AMPEDO
Wanton, farewell! I faint, Death's frozen hand
Congeals life's little river in my breast.
No man before his end is truly blest.

[Dies.

ANDELOCIA
O miserable, miserable soul!
Thus a foul life makes death to look more foul.

Re-enter LONGAVILLE and MONTROSE with a halter.

LONGAVILLE
Thus shall this golden purse divided be,
One day for you, another day for me.

MONTROSE
Of days anon, say, what determine you,
Shall they have liberty, or shall they die?

LONGAVILLE
Die sure: and see, I think the elder's dead.

ANDELOCIA
Ay, murderers, he is dead. O sacred Wisdom,
Had Fortunatus been enamourèd
Of thy celestial beauty, his two sons
Had shined like two bright suns.

LONGAVILLE
Pull hard, Montrose.

ANDELOCIA
Come you to strangle me? are you the hangman?
Hell-hounds, y'are damned for this impiety.
Fortune, forgive me! I deserve thy hate;
Myself have made myself a reprobate.
Virtue, forgive me! for I have transgressed
Against thy laws; my vows are quite forgot,
And therefore shame is fallen to my sin's lot.
Riches and knowledge are two gifts divine.
They that abuse them both as I have done,
To shame, to beggary, to hell must run.
O conscience, hold thy sting, cease to afflict me.
Be quick, tormentors, I desire to die;
No death is equal to my misery.
Cyprus, vain world and vanity, farewell.
Who builds his Heaven on earth, is sure of hell.

[Dies.

LONGAVILLE
He's dead: in some deep vault let's throw their bodies.

MONTROSE
First let us see the purse, Lord Longaville.

LONGAVILLE
Here 'tis, by this we'll fill this tower with gold.

MONTROSE
Frenchman, this purse is counterfeit.

LONGAVILLE
Thou liest.
Scot, thou hast cozened me, give me the right,
Else shall thy bosom be my weapon's grave.

MONTROSE
Villain, thou shalt not rob me of my due.

[They fight.

Enter ATHELSTANE, AGRIPYNE, ORLEANS, GALLOWAY, CORNWALL, CHESTER, LINCOLN, and SHADOW with weapons at one door: FORTUNE, VICE, and their Attendants at the other.

ALL

Lay hands upon the murderers, strike them down.

FORTUNE
Surrender up this purse, for this is mine.

ALL
Are these two devils, or some powers divine?

SHADOW
O see, see, O my two masters, poor Shadow's substances; what shall I do? Whose body shall Shadow now follow?

FORTUNE
Peace, idiot, thou shalt find rich heaps of fools,
That will be proud to entertain a shadow.
I charm thy babbling lips from troubling me.
You need not hold them, see, I smite them down
Lower than hell: base souls, sink to your heaven.

VICE
I do arrest you both my prisoners.

FORTUNE
Stand not amazed, you gods of earth, at this,
She that arresteth these two fools is Vice,
They have broke Virtue's laws, Vice is her sergeant,
Her jailer and her executioner.
Look on those Cypriots, Fortunatus' sons,
They and their father were my minions,
My name is Fortune.

ALL
O dread deity!

FORTUNE
Kneel not to me: if Fortune list to frown,
You need not fall down, for she'll spurn you down;
Arise! but, fools, on you I'll triumph thus:
What have you gained by being covetous?
This prodigal purse did Fortune's bounteous hand
Bestow on them, their riots made them poor,
And set these marks of miserable death
On all their pride, the famine of base gold
Hath made your souls to murder's hands be sold,
Only to be called rich. But, idiots, see
The virtues to be fled, Fortune hath caused it so;
Those that will all devour, must all forego.

ATHELSTANE
Most sacred Goddess!

FORTUNE
Peace, you flatterer.
Thy tongue but heaps more vengeance on thy head.
Fortune is angry with thee, in thee burns
A greedy covetous fire, in Agripyne
Pride like a monarch revels, and those sins
Have led you blind-fold to your former shames,
But Virtue pardoned you, and so doth Fortune.

ATHELSTANE and AGRIPYNE
All thanks to both your sacred deities.

FORTUNE
As for these metal-eaters, these base thieves,
Who rather than they would be counted poor,
Will dig through hell for gold,—you were forgiven
By Virtue's general pardon; her broad seal
Gave you your lives, when she took off your horns.
Yet having scarce one foot out of the jail,
You tempt damnation by more desperate means,
You both are mortal, and your pains shall ring
Through both your ears, to terrify your souls,
As please the judgment of this mortal king.

ATHELSTANE
Fair Empress of the world, since you resign
Your power to me, this sentence shall be mine:
Thou shall be tortured on a wheel to death,
Thou with wild horses shall be quarterèd.

[Points to MONTROSE and LONGAVILLE.

VICE
Ha, ha, weak judge, weak judgment; I reverse
That sentence, for they are my prisoners.
Embalm the bodies of those Cypriots,
And honour them with princely burial.
For those do as you please; but for these two,
I kiss you both, I love you, y'are my minions.
Untie their bands, Vice doth reprieve you both.
I set you free.

BOTH
Thanks, gracious deity.

VICE
Begone, but you in liberty shall find
More bondage than in chains; fools, get you hence,
Both wander with tormented conscience.

LONGAVILLE
O horrid judgment, that's the hell indeed.

MONTROSE
Come, come, our death ne'er ends if conscience bleed.

BOTH
O miserable, miserable men!

[Exeunt LONGAVILLE and MONTROSE.

FORTUNE
Fortune triumphs at this, yet to appear
All like myself, that which from those I took,
King Athelstane, I will bestow on thee,
And in it the old virtue I infuse:
But, king, take heed how thou my gifts dost use.
England shall ne'er be poor, if England strive
Rather by virtue than by wealth to thrive.

Enter VIRTUE, crowned: NYMPHS and KINGS attending on her, crowned with olive branches and laurels; music sounding.

VICE
Virtue? alas good soul, she hides her head.

VIRTUE
What envious tongue said, "Virtue hides her head?"

VICE
She that will drive thee into banishment.

FORTUNE
She that hath conquered thee: how dar'st thou come,
Thus tricked in gaudy feathers, and thus guarded
With crownèd kings and Muses, when thy foe
Hath trod thus on thee, and now triumphs so?
Where's virtuous Ampedo? See, he's her slave;
For following thee, this recompense they have.

VIRTUE
Is Ampedo her slave? Why, that's my glory.
The idiot's cap I once wore on my head,

Did figure him; those that like him do muffle
Virtue in clouds, and care not how she shine,
I'll make their glory like to his decline.
He made no use of me, but like a miser,
Locked up his wealth in rusty bars of sloth;
His face was beautiful, but wore a mask,
And in the world's eyes seemed a blackamoor:
So perish they that so keep Virtue poor.

VICE
Thou art a fool to strive, I am more strong,
And greater than thyself; then, Virtue, fly,
And hide thy face, yield me the victory.

VIRTUE
Is Vice higher than Virtue? that's my glory,
The higher that thou art, thou art more horrid:
The world will love me for my comeliness.

FORTUNE
Thine own self loves thyself: why on the heads
Of Agripyne, Montrose, and Longaville,—
English, Scot, French—did Vice clap ugly horns,
But to approve that English, French and Scot,
And all the world else, kneel and honour Vice;
But in no country, Virtue is of price!

VIRTUE
Yes, in all countries Virtue is of price,
In every kingdom some diviner breast
Is more enamoured of me than the rest.
Have English, Scot and French bowed knees to thee?
Why that's my glory too, for by their shame,
Men will abhor thee and adore my name.
Fortune, thou art too weak, Vice, th'art a fool
To fight with me; I suffered you awhile
T'eclipse my brightness, but I now will shine,
And make you swear your beauty's base to mine.

FORTUNE
Thou art too insolent; see, here's a court
Of mortal judges; let's by them be tried,
Which of us three shall most be deified.

VICE
I am content.

FORTUNE

And I.

VIRTUE
So am not I.
My judge shall be your sacred deity.[76]

[76] Virtue here evidently addressed Queen Elizabeth, as she sat in the audience; this direct recognition is kept up to the end of the play.

VICE
O miserable me, I am undone.

[Exit VICE and her train.

ALL
O stop the horrid monster.

VIRTUE
Let her run.
Fortune, who conquers now?

FORTUNE
Virtue, I see,
Thou wilt triumph both over her and me.

All. Empress of Heaven and earth.

FORTUNE
Why do you mock me?
Kneel not to me, to her transfer your eyes,
There sits the Queen of Chance, I bend my knees
Lower than yours. Dread goddess, 'tis most meet
That Fortune fall down at thy conquering feet.
Thou sacred Empress that command'st the Fates,
Forgive what I have to thy handmaid done,
And at thy chariot wheels Fortune shall run,
And be thy captive, and to thee resign
All powers which Heaven's large patent have made mine.

VIRTUE
Fortune, th'art vanquished. Sacred deity,
O now pronounce who wins the victory,
And yet that sentence needs not, since alone,
Your virtuous presence Vice hath overthrown,
Yet to confirm the conquest on your side,
Look but on Fortunatus and his sons;
Of all the wealth those gallants did possess,
Only poor Shadow is left, comfortless:

Their glory's faded and their golden pride.

SHADOW
Only poor Shadow tells how poor they died.

VIRTUE
All that they had, or mortal men can have,
Sends only but a Shadow from the grave.
Virtue alone lives still, and lives in you;
I am a counterfeit, you are the true;
I am a shadow, at your feet I fall,
Begging for these, and these, myself and all.
All these that thus do kneel before your eyes,
Are shadows like myself: dread nymph, it lies
In you to make us substances. O do it!
Virtue I am sure you love, she wooes you to it.
I read a verdict in your sun-like eyes,
And this it is: Virtue the victory.

ALL
All loudly cry, Virtue the victory!

FORTUNE
Virtue the victory! for joy of this,
Those self-same hymns which you to Fortune sung
Let them be now in Virtue's honour rung.

SONG.

Virtue smiles: cry holiday,
Dimples on her cheeks do dwell,
Virtue frowns, cry welladay,
Her love is Heaven, her hate is hell.
Since Heaven and hell obey her power,
Tremble when her eyes do lower.
Since Heaven and hell her power obey,
Where she smiles, cry holiday.

Holiday with joy we cry,
And bend, and bend, and merrily,
Sing hymns to Virtue's deity:
Sing hymns to Virtue's deity.

As they are about to depart, enter TWO OLD MEN.

THE EPILOGUE AT COURT.[77]

[77] See note 1 to Prologue.

1st OLD MAN
Nay stay, poor pilgrims, when I entered first
The circle of this bright celestial sphere,
I wept for joy, now I could weep for fear.

2nd OLD MAN
I fear we all like mortal men shall prove
Weak, not in love, but in expressing love.

1st OLD MAN
Let every one beg once more on his knee,
One pardon for himself, and one for me;
For I enticed you hither. O dear Goddess,
Breathe life in our numbed spirits with one smile,
And from this cold earth, we with lively souls,
Shall rise like men new-born, and make Heaven sound
With hymns sung to thy name, and prayers that we
May once a year so oft enjoy this sight,
Till these young boys change their curled locks to white,
And when gray-wingèd age sits on their heads,
That so their children may supply their steads,
And that Heaven's great arithmetician,
Who in the scales of number weighs the world,
May still to forty-two add one year more,
And still add one to one, that went before,
And multiply four tens by many a ten:
To this I cry, Amen.

ALL
Amen, amen!

1st OLD MAN
Good-night, dear mistress, those that wish thee harm,
Thus let them stoop under destruction's arm.

ALL
Amen, amen, amen!

[Exeunt.

Thomas Dekker – A Short Biography

Thomas Dekker was born around 1572, there is no certainty as to date and it is only probable that he was born in London. Little is known of his early years. From such an unknown start he was however to make quite a name for himself.

By the mid 1590s Dekker had set forth on a career as a playwright. Samples of his work (though not the actual date) can be found in the manuscript of Sir Thomas More. Of more certainty is work as a playwright for the Admiral's Men of Philip Henslowe, in whose records of account he is first mentioned in early 1598.

While there are plays connected with his name performed as early as 1594, it is not clear that he was the original author or part of a team involved in revising and updating. Much of his work has been lost and whilst his prolific output argues against any uniform quality there are undoubted gems both as a solo writer and as part of various collaborations. Indeed between 1598 and 1602, about forty plays for Henslowe, usually in collaboration, can be attributed to him.

Dekker's name first appears in Henslowe's diary* in connection with "fayeton" (presumably, Phaeton) in 1598. There follow, before 1599, payments for work on The Triplicity of Cuckolds, The Mad Man's Morris, and Hannibal and Hermes. He worked on these plays with Robert Wilson, Henry Chettle, and Michael Drayton. With Drayton, he also worked on history plays on the French civil wars, Earl Godwin, and others.

It is also recorded at this time that Dekker's long association with financial mishaps was going to be a life-long concern. He was imprisoned for a short time for debt in Poultry Compter, a small prison run by the Sherriff of London. It was used to house prisoners such as vagrants, debtors and religious dissenters, as well as criminals convicted of misdemeanours including homosexuality, prostitution and drunkenness.

In 1599, he wrote plays on Troilus and Cressida, Agamemnon (with Chettle), and Page of Plymouth. In that year, also, he collaborated with Chettle, Jonson, and Marston on a play about Robert II.

1599 also saw the production of three plays that have survived including his most famous work, The Shoemaker's Holiday, or the Gentle Craft. This play reflects the daily lives of ordinary Londoners, and contains the poem The Merry Month of May. The play reflects the trend for the intermingling of everyday subjects with the fantastical, embodied here by the rise of a craftsman to Mayor and the involvement of an unnamed but idealised king in the concluding banquet. Old Fortunatus and Patient Grissel are the two other surviving plays.

In 1600, he worked on The Seven Wise Masters, Fortune's Tennis, Cupid and Psyche, and Fair Constance of Rome. The next year, in addition to the classic Satiromastix, he worked on a play possibly about Sebastian of Portugal and Blurt, Master Constable, on which he may have collaborated with Thomas Middleton.

To these years also belong the collaborations with Ben Jonson and John Marston, which presumably contributed to the War of the Theatres in 1600 and 1601. To Jonson, Dekker was a hack, a "dresser of plays about town"; Jonson made fun of Dekker as Demetrius Fannius in Poetaster and as Anaides in Cynthia's Revels.

Dekker's riposte, Satiromastix, performed both by the Lord Chamberlain's Men and the child actors of Paul's, casts Jonson as an affected, hypocritical Horace and marks the end of the "poetomachia".

In 1602 he revised two older plays, Pontius Pilate (1597) and the second part of Sir John Oldcastle. He also collaborated on Caesar's Fall, Jephthah, A Medicine for a Curst Wife, Sir Thomas Wyatt (on Wyatt's rebellion), and Christmas Comes But Once a Year.

By 1603, Jonson and Dekker collaborated again, on a pageant for the Royal Entry, delayed from the coronation of James I, for which Dekker also wrote the festival book The Magnificent Entertainment.

At this point Dekker becomes more interested in writing pamphlets; he had done so from the start of his career but now increases his work flow and his playwriting output noticeably declines. It appears also that his association with Henslowe also breaks at this point.

In Dekker's first rush of pamphleteering, in 1603, was The Wonderful Year, a journalistic account of the death of Elizabeth, accession of James I, and the 1603 plague, that combined a wide variety of literary styles to convey the extraordinary events of that year ('wonderful' here meaning astonishing). Its reception prompted two more plague pamphlets, News From Gravesend and The Meeting of Gallants at an Ordinary. The Double PP (1606) is an anti-Catholic tract written in response to the Gunpowder Plot. News From Hell (1606) is an homage to and continuation of Nash's Pierce Penniless. The Seven Deadly Sins of London (1606) continues the plague pamphlet series.

In 1604, he and Middleton wrote The Honest Whore for the Fortune, and Dekker contributed a sequel himself the following year. The Middleton/Dekker collaboration The Family of Love also dates from this time. Dekker and Webster also wrote Westward Ho and Northward Ho for Paul's Boys.

The failures of The Whore of Babylon (1607) and If This Be Not a Good Play, the Devil is in It (1611) left him crestfallen; the latter play was rejected by Prince Henry's Men before failing for Queen Anne's Men at the Red Bull Theatre.

After 1608, Dekker produced his most popular pamphlets: a series of "cony-catching" pamphlets that described the various tricks and deceits of confidence-men and thieves, including Thieves' Cant. These pamphlets, which Dekker often updated and reissued, include The Belman of London (1608, now The Bellman of London), Lanthorne and Candle-light, Villainies Discovered by Candlelight, and English Villainies. They owe their form and many of their incidents to similar pamphlets by Robert Greene.

Other pamphlets are journalistic in form and offer vivid pictures of Jacobean London. The Dead Term (1608) describes Westminster during summer vacation. The Guls Horne-Booke (1609, now The Gull's Hornbook) describes the life of city gallants, with a valuable account of behaviour in the London theatres. Work for Armourers (1609) and The Artillery Garden (1616) (the latter in verse) describe aspects of England's military industries. London Look Back (1630) treats 1625, the year of James's death, while Wars, Wars, Wars (1628) describes European turmoil.

The Roaring Girl, a city comedy that using the real-life figure 'Moll Cutpurse', aka Mary Frith, was another collaboration with Middleton in 1611. The same year, he wrote another tragicomedy; Match Me in London.

In 1612, Dekker's lifelong problem with debt reached a crisis point when he was imprisoned in the King's Bench Prison on a debt of forty pounds to the father of John Webster. He remained there for seven years and continued writing pamphlets during these years but wrote no plays. He did however contribute six prison-based sketches to the sixth edition (1616) of Sir Thomas Overbury's Characters; and he revised Lanthorne and Candlelight to reflect what he had learned in prison.

Dekker also wrote a long poem Dekker His Dreame (1620) cataloguing his despairing confinement;

After his release, he collaborated with Day on Guy of Warwick (1620), The Wonder of a Kingdom (1623), and The Bellman of Paris (1623). He also wrote the tragicomedy The Noble Spanish Soldier (1622) and later reworked material from this play into a comedic form to produce The Welsh Ambassador (1623).

With John Ford, he wrote The Sun's Darling (1624), The Fairy Knight (1624), and The Bristow Merchant (1624).

Another play, The Late Murder of the Son upon the Mother, or Keep the Widow Waking (with Ford, Webster, and William Rowley) dramatized two recent murders in Whitechapel, and resulted in a suit for slander heard in the Star Chamber.

Dekker turned once more to pamphlet-writing, revamping old work and writing a new preface to his most popular tract, The Bellman of London.

Dekker's plays of the 1620s were staged at the large amphitheaters on the north side of London, most commonly at the Red Bull; only two of his later plays were seen at the more exclusive, indoor Cockpit Theatre. The Shoreditch amphitheaters had become identified with the louder, less reputable play-goers, such as apprentices. Dekker's type of play seems to have suited them perfectly. Full of bold action and complementary to the values and beliefs of such audiences, his drama carried much of the thrusting optimism of Elizabethan drama into the Caroline era.

Dekker published no more work after 1632, and he it is thought he died on August 25th, 1632, recorded as "Thomas Dekker, householder". He is buried at St. James's in Clerkenwell.

Most of Dekker's work is lost. His disordered life, and his lack of a firm connection (such as Shakespeare had) with a single company, may have hindered the preservation or publication of manuscripts although perhaps twenty of his plays were published during his lifetime.

****Henslowe's diary***
Philip Henslowe was an Elizabethan theatrical entrepreneur and impresario although he had a wide range of other business interests. Henslowe's reputation rests on the survival of his diary, a primary source for information about the theatrical world of Renaissance London.

Henslowe's "diary" is a valuable source on the theatrical history of the period. It is a collection of memoranda and notes that record payments to writers, box office takings, and lists of money lent. Also of interest are records of the purchase of expensive costumes and of stage properties, such as the dragon in Christopher Marlowe's Doctor Faustus, providing an insight into the staging of plays in the Elizabethan theatre.

The diary is written on the reverse of pages of a book of accounts of his brother-in-law Ralf Hogge's ironworks, kept by his brother John Henslowe for the period 1576–1581. Hogge was the Queen's Gunstone maker, and produced both iron cannon and shot for the Royal Armouries at the Tower of London. John Henslowe seems to have acted as his agent, and Philip to have prudently reused his old account book. Hence these entries are also a valuable source for the early iron-making industry.

The diary begins with Henslowe's theatrical activities for 1592. Entries, with varying degrees of detail (authors' names were not included before 1597), until 1609. In the years before his death, Henslowe appears to have run his theatrical interests from a greater distance.

The diary records payments to twenty-seven Elizabethan playwrights. He variously commissioned, bought and produced plays by, or made loans to Ben Jonson, Christopher Marlowe, Thomas Middleton, Robert Greene, Henry Chettle, George Chapman, Thomas Dekker, John Webster, Anthony Munday, Henry Porter, John Day, John Marston and Michael Drayton. The diary reveals the varying partnerships between writers, in an age when many plays were collaborations. It also shows Henslowe to have been a careful man of business, obtaining security in the form of rights to his authors' works, and holding their manuscripts, while tying them to him with loans and advances. If a play was successful, Henslowe would commission a sequel.

Performances of works with titles similar to Shakespearean plays, such as a Hamlet, a Henry VI, Part 1, a Henry V, a The Taming of the Shrew and a Titus Andronicus are mentioned in the diary with no author listed. Most of these plays were recorded when the Admiral's Men and the Lord Chamberlain's Men briefly joined forces when the playhouses were closed owing to the plague (June 1594).

In 1599, Henslowe paid Dekker and Henry Chettle for a play called Troilus and Cressida, which is probably the play currently known as British Museum MS. Add 10449 (the actors' names that appear in the plot connect it to the Admiral's Men and date it between March 1598 and July 1600). There is no mention of William Shakespeare (or for that matter Richard Burbage) in Henslowe's diary (despite the forgeries of John Payne Collier), this is due to the fact that Shakespeare and Burbage were during most of their career not connected to Henslowe's theatre, Shakespeare's company, the Lord Chamberlain's Men, performed at The Theatre (starting in 1594) and later The Globe Theatre (starting in 1599).

Thomas Dekker – A Concise Bibliography

Plays – Sole Authorship
The Shoemaker's Holiday (1599)
Old Fortunatus (1600)
The Noble Spanish Soldier (1602)
Troja-Nova Triumphans, or London Triumphing (1612)
London's Tempe; or, The Feild of Happines (1629)
The Honest Whore, Part II (1630)
Match Me in London (1631)
The Wonder of a Kingdom (1634)

Plays – Co-Written

Satiro-Mastix (1601) with Marston
Blurt, Master Constable (1602) with Middleton
Patient Grissill (1603) with Chettle and Haughton
The Honest Whore, Part I (1604) with Middleton
The Magnificent Entertainment (1604) with Jonson et al.
The Family of Love (1603-1607) with Middleton
Northward Ho (1607) with Webster
Westward Ho (1607) with Webster
The Famous History of Sir Thomas Wyatt (1607) with Webster
The Roaring Girl (1610) with Middleton
The Witch of Edmonton (1621) with Ford, Rowley, &c.
The Virgin-Martyr (1622) with Massinger
The Sun's Darling (1623-4) with Ford
The Bloody Banquet (1639) with Middleton

Non-Dramatic Works
The Wonderful Year (1603)
News from Hell (1606)
The Double PP (1606)
The Seven Deadly Sins of London (1606)
Jests to Make You Merry (1607)
The Bellman of London (1608)
Lanthorne and Candle-light (1608)
The Dead Term (1608)
The Gull's Hornbook (1609)
The Four Birds of Noah's Ark (1609)
The Raven's Almanack (1609)
Work for Armourers (1609)
O Per Se O (1612)
A Strange Horse-Race (1613)
Dekker, His Dreame (1620)
A Rod for Runaways (1625)

Poems
Golden Slumbers Kiss Your Eyes
Beauty Arise
Cast Away Care
The Invitation
Fancies Are But Streams
Here Lies The Blithe Spring

www.ingramcontent.com/pod-product-compliance
Lightning Source LLC
Chambersburg PA
CBHW071304040426
42444CB00009B/1862